QUEERING AUTOETHNOGRAPHY

Queering Autoethnography articulates for the first time the possibilities and politics of queering autoethnography, both in theoretical terms and as an intervention into narratives and cultures of apology, shame and fear. Despite the so-called mainstreaming of same-sex relationships and trans★ visibility, many within gender's 'liminal zone' remain invisible and unrecognized, existing somewhere outside of heteronormative relationships and institutions. At the same time, the political and scholarly potential of autoethnography is expanding, particularly in its ability to evoke empathic and affective responses at a time of public numbness, a practice crucial to making scholarly research relevant to the work of global citizenship and crafting meaningful lives.

This volume considers flash points in contemporary scholarly and popular culture such as queer memorializing and mourning; unintelligibility and monstrosity; physical, digital and cultural transformations of queer lives and bodies; the power and danger wrought in the public assembly of queer people in a culture of massacre; and the promise of queer futurities in the contemporary moment. It also makes original theoretical contributions that include concepts such as *massacre culture*, *queer terror*, *mundane annihilations* and *activist affect*. We write these ideas in action, joining theory and story as a contact zone for analysis, critique and change.

Stacy Holman Jones is Professor in the Centre for Theatre and Performance at Monash University.

Anne M. Harris is Vice Chancellor's Principal Research Fellow and Associate Professor at RMIT University.

QUEERING AUTOETHNOGRAPHY

Stacy Holman Jones and Anne M. Harris

Routledge
Taylor & Francis Group

NEW YORK AND LONDON

First published 2019
by Routledge
711 Third Avenue, New York, NY 10017

and by Routledge
2 Park Square, Milton Park, Abingdon, Oxon, OX14 4RN

Routledge is an imprint of the Taylor & Francis Group, an informa business

© 2019 Taylor & Francis

Library of Congress Cataloging-in-Publication Data
Names: Holman Jones, Stacy Linn, 1966– author. | Harris, Anne M.,
    author.
Title: Queering autoethnography / Stacy Holman Jones and Anne M.
    Harris.
Description: New York : Routledge, 2019.
Identifiers: LCCN 2018020998 | ISBN 9781138286153 (hardback) |
    ISBN 9781138286160 (pbk.) | ISBN 9781315268590 (ebook)
Subjects: LCSH: Queer theory. | Ethnology—Authorship.
Classification: LCC HQ76.25 .H6425 2019 | DDC 306.7601—dc23
LC record available at https://lccn.loc.gov/2018020998

ISBN: 978-1-138-28615-3 (hbk)
ISBN: 978-1-138-28616-0 (pbk)
ISBN: 978-1-315-26859-0 (ebk)

Typeset in Bembo
by Apex CoVantage, LLC

Printed in the United Kingdom
by Henry Ling Limited

We dedicate this book to queer storytellers past and present who bravely, persistently and beautifully told their truths so that we may tell ours.

CONTENTS

ACKNOWLEDGMENTS

We both thank Hannah Shakespeare at Routledge who is the best editor ever. Thanks to Tony E. Adams who, with Stacy, originally conceived of this book, and to Mitch Allen for saying yes to it in Murphy's bar at the International Congress of Qualitative Inquiry (ICQI) so many years ago.

We also thank our critical autoethnography family at ICQI for the nurturing and sustaining community we've created over so many years, particularly Ron Pelias, Craig Gingrich-Philbrook, Devika Chawla, Jonathan Wyatt, Ken Gale, A.B., Robin Boylorn, Chris Poulos, Lesa Lockford, Bryant Alexander, Marcelo Diversi, Norm Denzin, Ken Gale, Claudio Moriera, Kitrina Douglas, Karen Werner, Glenn Phillips, Durell Callier, Dominique Hill, David Purnell, Deanna Shoemaker, Jenn Erdely, Tami Spry, Elyse Pineau and Sandra Faulkner.

We wish to thank our global south *Critical Autoethnography* family who demonstrate each year the power of public (and intimate) assembly, now in its fourth year: Liz Mackinlay, Fetaui Iosefo, Esther Fitzpatrick, Michael Crowhurst, Craig Wood, Kate Coleman, Geraldine Burke, Peta Murray, Julie Peters, Glen Parkes, Phiona Stanley, Yassir Morsi, Jack Migdalek and so many other beautiful writers and human beings.

Anne

I thank Stacy for inviting me into this much-needed book project that has become a labor of love. I am grateful for that fortuitous conversation over conference drinks with Tony E. Adams, Derek Bolen and Stacy, at which I rather overenthusiastically proposed *Critical Autoethnography* as a 'sister conference' to the *Doing Autoethnography* conference in San Angelo, Texas, and which has become a most sustaining critical autoethnography community of practice for me. Many thanks, too, to my colleagues at RMIT University School of Education, Digital

Ethnography Research Centre, and Design and Creative Practice platform for their creative practice scholarship, collaboration and community.

I thank Murphy and Tasha, our long-suffering dogs, for not running away from home after months and months (ok, let's face it: years and years) of distraction by their owners who only seem to care about books. I thank the Catholic Church and Catholic Charities (their adoption arm), whose death-making policies around queerness and adoption have given me so much rich loam for my autoethnographic writing throughout my life.

And as always, I thank you Stacy for your ever-curious heart regarding gender diversity, adoption, queerness, transcoding and other digital media experiments, and for saying *yes* when I invited you to fly across the globe as a visiting scholar all those days and nights ago. I thank you for reinforcing the life-affirming practice of writing against the grain, theorizing with love and creativity, ignoring the naysayers and humanizing academic work through turning stereotypes about 'mesearch' into the reworlding work of critical and queer autoethnography in times of terror. I thank you for the words and for the *morethanwords* affect with which you continue to enrich my life immeasurably.

Stacy

I would like to thank Nick Trujillo, Carolyn Ellis and Art Bochner, all of whom taught me about autoethnography and for whom storytelling was not only a way to account for the workings of emotions, embodiment, relationships and power in scholarship and the building of knowledge, but also a way of life and living.

I'd also like to thank Paul Gray, Omi Osun Joni L. Jones, Lynn Miller, Ann Daly and most of all Kathleen Stewart at the University of Texas for teaching me so well, and my colleagues at USF, CSUN and now in the Centre for Theatre and Performance at Monash University, Australia, for encouraging me in this work. I thank Norman Denzin for inviting me to write and speak and do autoethnography in myriad ways and venues.

I also thank Tony E. Adams, with whom I have written about and through queer autoethnography for more than a decade. I'm so glad you said yes to that first invitation to work together and that we continue, even now, to write where autoethnography might take us, together.

Most of all, I thank Anne Harris, without whom this book and this life would not be possible. On days when we sit at keyboards for too long, ignoring the dogs, your encouragement, your energy, your questions and the beautiful semblance of your words and ideas sustain me. The privilege of walking with you and the dogs along the water at sunset at the end of such busy days fills me, as Samuel L. Delaney writes, "with heart-thudding astonishment."

INTRODUCTION

Queering Autoethnography

It is fatal to be a man or woman pure and simple; one must be woman-manly or man-womanly . . . some marriage of opposites has to be consummated.

—(Woolf 1929/2001, p. 122)

The self is also a creation, the principal work of your life, the crafting of which makes everyone an artist. This unfinished work of becoming ends only when you do, if then, and the consequences live on. We make ourselves and in so doing are the gods of the small universe of self and the large world of repercussions.

—(Solnit 2016, p. 53)

Queering Methodology

A queer methodology, in a way, is a scavenger methodology that uses different methods to collect and produce information on subjects who have been deliberately or accidentally excluded from traditional studies of human behavior. The queer methodology attempts to combine methods that are often cast as being at odds with each other, and it refuses the academic compulsion toward disciplinary coherence.

—(Halberstam 1998, p. 13)

Autoethnography has emerged as a methodology of interest to qualitative scholars in fields including communication, education, performance studies, creative writing, psychology, sociology, social work, political science, anthropology cultural studies and more. This diverse and abiding commitment to autoethnography is due largely to its ability to bring together the concrete detail of the personal and the power of theoretical frameworks that help us understand how stories animate and become the change we seek in the world (Holman Jones 2016). The development of autoethnography is situated within a larger set of shifts and changes in qualitative (and post-qualitative) inquiry that followed the "crisis of representation" in anthropology and other disciplines (Marcus & Fischer 1999, Reed-Danahay 2002, Rosaldo 1989, Denzin & Lincoln 2005). This crisis radically shifted the purpose and practices of research in ways that not only recognized but embraced the limits of scientific knowledge, questioning the surety with which any research can make generalized and objective claims about people, objects, experience, relationships and cultures; the bias against affect, emotion and difference; prohibitions against including the researcher's voice, experience and storytelling as ways of knowing; and concerns about the ethics and politics of research and representation (Adams et al. 2015, pp. 8–12). At the same time, researchers were increasingly called upon to consider and account for relations and dynamics of power and difference not only in the world, but also in their research.

In anthropology, sociology and gender and sexualities studies (as well as in other disciplines), ethnographers reminded us of the necessity of understanding the individual in relation to culture and politics and bringing ethnographic research and representation back to the body itself, to corporeality and to a range of post-structural and postmodern approaches that understand the co-constitutive nature of performing self-in-culture. Autoethnographers responded to the shifts and concerns in qualitative research in general, and ethnography in particular, by placing equal importance on knowledge building and aesthetics; attending to the ethical and relational implications of their work for themselves, participants and readers/audiences; and connecting personal experience to institutional, political, social and interpersonal relationships of power (Adams et al. 2015, p. 25).

Investigating how experiences are enlarged and/or constrained by relations of power has been the particular focus of critical autoethnography and autoethnographers for whom the "responsibility to address processes of unfairness or injustice within a particular lived domain," including our own research, is paramount (Madison 2012, p. 5; see also Spry 2016, Boylorn & Orbe 2013). Focusing on experience within relationships of power asks autoethnographers to attend to intersectionality, a term coined by Kimberlé Crenshaw (1991) to call attention to how oppressive institutions, attitudes and actions in cultures including racism, xenophobia, sexism, heteronormativity, classism, religious and spiritual fundamentalism, ageism and ableism are connected and mutually influencing. Intersectional autoethnographies work to "capture the complexities of intersecting power relations" by producing multiple and diverse perspectives and voices (Hill Collins 2016, p. 135). Taking our cue from intersectional scholars and scholarship, critical autoethnographers seek firstly to problematize and question existing knowledge about culture and cultural experience by "analyzing socially unjust practices" (Hill Collins 2016, p. 135); secondly, to put critical theory into action by joining the social and political insights that critical theory offers us to the specific and concrete positions, places and people they originate for and from (Holman Jones 2017); and thirdly to build "new knowledge about the social world in order to stimulate new practices" for transformation (Hill Collins 2016, p. 135).

Similarly, queer and gender studies have entered a new period of critical application in ever-widening fields and conversations. Despite the so-called mainstreaming of same-sex relationships and trans★[1] visibility, many within gender's 'liminal zone' remain unintelligible, existing somewhere outside of heteronormative relationships and institutions. The recent mass shootings in the United States, the rollback of protections for lesbian, gay, bisexual, trans★, intersex and queer (LGBTIQ) persons worldwide (Diamond 2018, Crossley et al. 2017, "Action Needed," 2017) and the alarming increase in the numbers of crimes of violence and murder against trans★ subjects ("A Time to Act" 2017, Jung Thapa 2016) bears witness to the need to resist complacency in LGBTIQ rights and to remain committed to the critical project of queer and gender diversity studies.

Through the intersectional project of problematizing relationships of gender, sexuality and power, queer and gender studies have worked to displace heterosexuality as the normative mode and structure for gendered and sexual relationships, making an argument against gay and lesbian studies and politics as a single or monolithic project, and insisting that race critically shapes sexual identities ("Queer Theory"). Queer *theory* questions a singular notion or mode of 'queer' politics and mobilizes the insights of queer and gender studies in order to stimulate new and different practices, institutions and modes of being (see De Lauretis 1991, Sedgwick 1990, Butler 1990; see also Barker 2016, Ruffalo 2016, Haley & Parker 2011, Sullivan 2003 and Turner 2000).

The "queer" in queer theory, as Butler (1993) writes, is a "site of collective contestation, the point of departure for a set of historical reflections and future imaginings" (p. 220). Sara Ahmed (2006) reminds us of the origins of queer, from the Greek for "cross, oblique and adverse" and the implications of those origins for *being* queer, which highlights how we move "between sexual and social registers without flattening them or reducing them to a single line" (p. 161). Queer not only points to an activist stance toward the theorizing of (gay, lesbian, bi and in some instances intersex and trans★) identities and the workings of power, but also the relationally lived experience of queer as fluid and unfinished, playful and political. In this sense queer, as Butler (1993) writes, is "never fully known, claimed or owned, but instead that which is deployed, twisted and queered from a prior usage and in the direction of urgent and expanding political purposes" (p. 220).

More than writing the experience of queer lives and relationships, in this book we take up the call to queer experience as a politics of writing lives and research, including autoethnography. Where autoethnographers including Art Bochner and Carolyn Ellis (2016) have perhaps always thought of the work they were doing as a critical project aimed at both fighting for social justice and "queering of social science" (p. 59), the work of queer autoethnography is explicitly vocal about and focused on the critical mission of the work (2016, pp. 59, 61).

Queering autoethnography draws on the practices and politics of queer and queering to offer narrative and theoretical disruptions of taken-for-granted knowledges that continue to marginalize, oppress and/or take advantage of those of us who do not participate or find ourselves reflected in mainstream cultures and social structures—which includes research methodologies.

Sarah Ahmed's notion of queering and queering *practices* as a method of intervention that "disturbs the order of things" is helpful in understanding what queering autoethnography might mean and do (2006, p. 161). Queering practices include "counter-normative" relational and political orientations and modes of reproduction that break into and breakdown "hetero-directive culture" (Taylor & Snowdon 2014, p. 185). Ahmed points out that heterosexuality, as a "compulsory orientation," reproduces more than itself—it reproduces capital and whiteness, among other normative practices (p. 161). And because of this intersectionality, the disruption and "disorientation" of queer as a sexual orientation "queers more than sex," as "sexual disorientation slides quickly into social disorientation, as a disorientation in how things are arranged" (pp. 161–162). As a method of intervention in autoethnography, queering practices "disturb the order of things" by creating dissonance around what passes as 'normal' and 'normative,' appropriating and assembling languages, texts, beliefs and ways of living and loving in radical and liberating ways; working against that which passes as stable, coherent, certain and fixed; and performing how words, thoughts, feelings and affective forces work and matter in our relationships and our representations (Holman Jones 2016; see also Harris & Holman Jones 2017; Harris 2016a, 2016b; Holman Jones & Harris 2016, 2016b; Harris 2014; Holman Jones & Adams 2010a, 2010b; Adams & Holman Jones 2008, 2011).

Why move to disrupt and disorient a research practice that is still, for many if not most, at the margins? Because we believe that the political and scholarly potential of autoethnography is still very much emerging and expanding, particularly in its potential to both evoke empathic and affective responses at a time of public numbness, a practice crucial to making scholarly research relevant to the work of global citizenship (see, for example, Denzin & Giardina 2017). However, a strictly descriptive and emotional approach or singular focus on form as a means of repeating—and reproducing—any particular "type" of autoethnography—critical, analytical, performance or evocative—ignores in large part autoethnography's abundance, beauty and radical potential. What, for example, might autoethnography become as it delves into more-than-human accounts? What might be possible if autoethnography were able to flex its muscles in the fields of digital media, biomedicine, aged care, animal husbandry, deep space exploration or nanotechnologies?

Part of what's required of those of us who are interested in exploring these questions is a move away from traditional notions of what counts as 'valid' or 'useful' in research, which has been historically measured based on its use value for humankind, no matter what abuses we bring to the earth and countless ecosystems, including those of some human beings. We see autoethnography as a method poised to move beyond that narcissistic and disaffected frame and lead humankind to begin attending to and empathizing with the non- and more-than-human. What then might be possible? Could our exercise of empathy for the known become a rehearsal for empathy for the unknown, or even the unknowable? What if that empathy gave way to a recognition of the precariousness and vulnerability of the other that allows all of us—animal, vegetable and mineral—to live out the ethical responsibility to not harm one another? Could such an autoethnography create the conditions under which we might create not only livable but also more bountiful futures?

Queering autoethnography might enable us to consider these and other questions of possibility and responsibility, creating a mode of engagement that addresses the consequences of crafting life for those of us who have been systematically excluded from culture within the larger world of repercussions (Halberstam 1998, p. 13; Solnit 2016, p. 53). The enactment of the corporeal and affective in a queering of autoethnography might also suggest a more sustainable way forward in which the story of the self, suddenly (and not so suddenly) becomes the story of us, and the story of the least of us becomes—at long last—our own.

As part of the project of questioning the normative in autoethnography, we want to reopen the discussion of the antiteleological ethos of an autoethnography that sought to make *less intelligible* a rigid research environment in which matters of autobiography were elided from scholarship about culture, as if those two performances were ever not interdependent (Bochner & Ellis 2016, p. 59). From its beginnings, autoethnography sought to challenge temporal and geographical and biographical claims and objectivities, in favor of a queer power of subjectivity in which the self was the only (if shifting) lens through which one could see.

This book asks for a return to some of the core challenges of autoethnography that look more toward our own becoming than legitimizing, measuring, characterizing and policing in relation to the academy and whatever we imagine 'academic work' to be: we return to the antiteleological potential of autoethnography in the doing of queer theory work, embracing a risky autoethnography that is inherently critical and intersectional, that is tethered as it must be to current events and challenges historical accounts; that undergoes a rigorous process of personal as well as critical interrogation in its efforts to be both transformative as well as deeply ethical. We return by recognizing the need to continually renew, and to discard the armor and protections we struggle under as we navigate everyday life, including methodologies. To take a not-strictly-autoethnographic example from Lev Manovich's (2001) work on cultural anxiety in response to the unforeclosed nature of contemporary digital life, a narrative from author Rick Moody (on the death of his sister) lays bare this sensibility:

> I should fictionalise it more, I should conceal myself. I should consider the responsibilities of characterization, I should conflate her two children into one, or reverse their genders, or otherwise alter them, I should make her boyfriend a husband, I should explicate all the tributaries of my extended family (its remarriages, its internecine politics), I should novelize the whole thing, I should make it multigenerational, I should work in my forefathers (stonemasons and newspapermen), I should let artifice create an elegant surface, I should make the events orderly, I should wait and write about it later, I should wait until I'm not angry, I shouldn't clutter a narrative with fragments, with mere recollections of good times, or with regrets, I should make Meredith's death shapely and persuasive, not blunt and disjunctive, I shouldn't' have to think the unthinkable, I shouldn't have to suffer, I should address her here directly (these are the ways I miss you), I should write only of affection, I should make our travels in this earthly landscape safe and secure, I should have a better ending, I shouldn't say her life was short and often sad, I shouldn't say she had demons, as I do too.
>
> *(qtd. in Manovich 2001, p. 44)*

In addition to the instability of any subject position, including the "I" and the wavering methodological dance of Moody's "shoulds," we return to questioning how the idealizations of objective knowing are communicated as methodological certainties. Take, for example, Craig Gingrich-Philbrook's (2015) meditation on the familiar advice in autoethnography that one should avoid writing about (difficult, complex, challenging) experience "too soon" after that experience to be safe for the writer, or the reader, or the constructions of "objective" claims that depend on the "conflation of knowledge and time" (p. 201). Trying to live up to these methodological certainties and admonitions "crowds out the compelling imperfection of the humanity that persists, unrecognized in their shadow until it dies for lack of our acknowledgment," as well as the understanding that even the most "centered and still of our reflections is impermanent" (p. 201). Waiting to write until we are "ready to write" a certain and knowledgeable account, Gingrich-Philbrook notes, "doesn't happen at a pre-extant arrival gate we finally discover. Rather, we conjure that moment of arrival in an act of perception we might later revise" (p. 202). Writing out of and through the dislocation and "becoming-time" of experience asks us, instead, to remain "chronically open" to risk, to a lack (or the opposite) of closure, and the something more and something else that inheres in that opening, that offer (pp. 201, 202).

From Me-Search to We-Search

For us, queering autoethnography is an offer to difference, to disorienting and disrupting, to impermanence and change, to expansion, to disruption and to new ontologies. We draw on post-structuralist frameworks, as well as postcolonial and new materialist approaches, in inviting readers to consider an autoethnography that can (and wants to) be untethered from the material, the biological, the foreclosed. Because of this, our book is not a how-to manual for autoethnographers seeking to write lesbian, gay, bisexual, intersex or trans★ subjectivities or experience. Instead, it is an intersectional, disruptive and disorienting intervention into normativity, precariousness and death-making politics and actions through the always already political project of autoethnography. We hope, through deployment of queering practices and the call more generally to put critical theory into action as a means of mobilizing change and transforming futures, to put to rest the now rather tiresome questioning of autoethnography as a rigorous and legitimate approach to scholarly research, including the glib dismissal of our work as *me*-search.

We make this intervention by exploding preconceptions about what it means to write-the-self-in-culture, while at the same time holding on to the necessity and indeed political power of acknowledging subjectivity and the limits of culture in contemporary research. What could be more necessary in these times of terror and loss?

Feminist Carol Hanisch's long-ago rallying cry "the personal is political" is never more necessary in a contemporary social and cultural landscape where questions of whose lives matter and whose lives "count as lives" are subject to debate (Hanisch 1969/2006, Butler 2006). We believe this accounts for some of the rapidly rising interest in autoethnography not only as a performative and reflexive form of critical research, but also as a way to find and make community in this time of fractured, individualized and atomizing culture. This is because autoethnography is a thoroughly *relational* practice, one concerned with and responsible for creating a dialog with a community of 'others,' rather than a monologue in which a "single and unified subject declares its will" (Butler 2015, p. 156). That, perhaps, is 'me-search,' but it is not autoethnography. Autoethnography is invested, instead, in 'we-search.' In other words, the work of autoethnography is the work of "assembling a we," a community of thinkers and writers and performers committed to speaking and embodying a collective and popular "will" (Butler 2015, p. 156; see also Holman Jones 2017). The collective and popular will of *this* book is an exploration of the radical potential of autoethnography as a (self-)critical and utopian heuristic for not only persisting but flourishing in contemporary terrorist/terrorized culture. By queering autoethnography, we are queering ourselves and others and culture, and in that queering we are—painfully, idealistically, reliably, finally—one.

This Book

Our book moves through a series of contexts in which autoethnography is queering contemporary global culture/s, and in turn how autoethnography is being queered. We expand a number of "complex and uncertain" theoretical concepts that "fascinate because they literally hit us or exert a pull on us" (Stewart 2007, p. 4): memorializing and mourning, readiness potential, public assembly, apocalypsis and precarity, transcoding, animacy and aliveness, intelligibility and queer futurities. The book also makes original theoretical contributions that include concepts such as *massacre culture, queer terror, mundane annihilations* and *activist affect*. We show these ideas "in action" in and on the narratives we create, aiming to "do theory and think story" as a way to "create a contact zone for analysis," critique and change (Pollock 2005, p. 1; Stewart 2007, p. 5).

In Chapter 1, Queering Monuments, we consider how words build a monument to queer lives and bodies through story (Solnit 2016), not only LTBTIQ memorializing in the wake of AIDS and trans and homophobic violence, but also in the insistence that the work of mourning invites us to imagine the future to come (O'Rourke 2014).

Chapter 2, Queering Massacres, takes up notions of precarity and what constitutes a grievable life, public assembly, an affective politics of "doing" and "feeling" queer and environmental disasters and toxic animacies (Berlant 2007; Butler 2006, 2009, 2015; Muñoz 2006; Chen 2011, 2012) to consider how queer bodies gathering in space performatively and politically enact a 'we' amidst the historical and environmental violence of massacre culture. We ask how the focus on the personal in the wake of atrocities might move autoethnography from a focus on individual stories of tragedies to a collective call for justice.

The idea of queer futurities and utopias (Halberstam 2005) in relation to current social movements and activism is our focus in Chapter 3, Queering Movements. We ask what an *activist affect* might be, and how it and autoethnography might inform social movements. We ask too what a persistent, resistant and insistent new queer story might do to imagine a future that is promised (and promising), but not yet here (Muñoz 2009).

Taking as a starting point the notion of 'vitality affect,' or the here-and-now 'eventfulness' of even the most mundane acts (Stern 1985, 2010; Massumi 2017), Chapter 4, Queering Mx, builds on Lev Manovich's (2001) concept of 'transcoding' in media ecologies. We consider transcoding as a queering of/by bodies and subjectivities that creates a vitally affective composite or 'queer Mx' body-subject. Here transcoding is a "body in code, a body whose embodiment is increasingly realized in conjunction with techniques" (Hansen 2006, p. 20). This chapter offers a queer lens for re/tooling, re/presenting and resisting staid and stable autoethnographic accounts through deployment of the gender-resistant identifier Mx, a transformation of the queer (cultural) autoethnographic body-subject.

Chapter 5, Queering Monsters, is an exploration of the often-monstrous unintelligibility of non-binary gender and sexual identifications and the monstrous narrative as a way of writing ourselves out of the 'bind' of gender binaries, heteronormative desires and traditional forms of kinship (Butler 2014; Holman Jones & Harris 2016).

Lastly, Chapter 6, Queering Memory, considers adoption and queerness as a queering of our ideas about memory and the possibility of a 'return' to experience as autoethnography in some way claims to do. For adoptees and for queer people, family is both virtual and actual: actual because presumably all of us have come from somewhere and someone; virtual because for adoptees and queer people, family is something that accrues over time and temporality lets us down. We can never go home, can never return. And yet, pulled by nostalgia and the limits of memory, we do return, again, rifling through the past looking for what's missing in love and families and home, to build another kind of love, kinship and memory.

Taken together, the chapters in *Queering Autoethnography* explore the challenging terrain of non-assimilationist narratives of gender and sexuality, worldmaking and remembrance, politics and family. We write at and into flash points in contemporary scholarly and popular culture such as using story to build queer monuments in the space cleared by violence against queer lives and bodies; the power and danger wrought in the public assembly of queer people in massacre culture; the promise of queer movements and futurities in the contemporary moment; physical, digital and cultural transformations of queer lives and bodies; queer unintelligibility and monstrosity; and the importance of queer memory and a return to the experiences that have touched our becoming, including most powerfully home and family. *Queering Autoethnography* articulates the contemporary political project of queer autoethnography, not only in theoretical terms but also as means for assembling a community invested in disrupting and changing narratives and cultures of apology, shame and fear. And so, for those who have been forgotten, lost, left behind, unacknowledged, hurt or silenced or worse: *Queer Autoethnography* is for us.

Note

1   We use the inclusive term *trans** to represent all those on the gender nonconforming spectrum.

References

A time to act: Fatal violence against transgender people in America, 2017. (2017). *Human rights campaign*. http://assets2.hrc.org/files/assets/resources/A_Time_To_Act_2017_REV3.pdf

Action needed to stop violations of LGBT people's rights worldwide, expert tells UN. (2017, 27 October). *UN News*. https://news.un.org/en/story/2017/10/569492-action-needed-stop-violations-lgbt-peoples-rights-worldwide-expert-tells-un

Adams, T.E. & Holman Jones, S. (2008). Autoethnography is queer. In Denzin, N.K., Lincoln, Y.S. & Smith, L.T., eds., *Handbook of critical and indigenous methodologies*, pp. 373–390. Thousand Oaks, CA: Sage.

Adams, T.E. & Holman Jones, S. (2011). Telling stories: Reflexivity, queer theory, and autoethnography. *Cultural Studies <-> Critical Methodologies*, 11(2), 108–116.

Adams, T.E., Holman Jones, S. & Ellis, C. (2015). *Autoethnography*. Oxford: Oxford University Press.

Ahmed, S. (2006). *Queer phenomenology: Orientations, objects, others*. Durham, NC: Duke University Press.

Barker, M.J. (2016). *Queer: A graphic history*. London: Icon.

Berlant, L. (2007). Slow death (sovereignty, obesity, lateral agency). *Critical Inquiry*, 33(4), 754–780.

Bochner, A. & Ellis, C. (2016). *Evocative autoethnography: Writing lives and telling stories*. New York and London: Routledge.

Boylorn, R.M. & Orbe, M.P. (eds.) (2013). *Critical autoethnography: Intersecting critical identities in everyday life*. Walnut Creek, CA: Left Coast Press.

Butler, J. (1990). *Gender trouble: Feminism and the subversion of identity*. New York: Routledge.

Butler, J. (1993). *Bodies that matter: On the discursive limits of "sex."* New York: Routledge.

Butler, J. (2006). *Precarious life: The power of mourning and violence*. New York: Verso.

Butler, J. (2009). *Frames of war: When is life grievable?* Brooklyn, NY: Verso.

Butler, J. (2014). Afterword. Animating autobiography: Barbara Johnson and Mary Shelley's Monster. In Johnson, B., ed., *A life with Mary Shelley*, pp. 37–50. Palo Alto, CA: Stanford University Press.

Butler, J. (2015). *Notes toward a performative theory of assembly*. Cambridge, MA: Harvard University Press.

Chen, M.Y. (2011). Toxic animacies, inanimate affections. *GLQ: A Journal of Lesbian and Gay Studies*, 17(2–3), 265–286.

Chen, M.Y. (2012). *Animacies: Biopolitics, racial mattering, and queer affect*. Durham, NC and London: Duke University Press.

Crenshaw, K. (1991). Mapping the margins: Intersectionality, identity politics, and violence against women of color. *Stanford Law Review*, 43, 1241–1299.

Crossley, P., Gourlay, C. & Spraggon, B. (2017, 15 November). Pride, prejudice and punishment: Gay rights around the world. *ABC News*. www.abc.net.au/news/2017-03-04/gay-lesbian-mardi-gras-rights-around-the-world/8126828.

De Lauretis, T. (1991). *Queer theory: Lesbian and gay sexualities*. Bloomington, IN: Indiana University Press.

Denzin, N.K. & Giardina, M.D. (2017). *Qualitative inquiry in neoliberal times*. New York and London: Routledge.

Denzin, N.K. & Lincoln, Y. (eds.) (2005). *Handbook of qualitative research*, 4th ed. Thousand Oaks, CA: Sage.

Diamond, D. (2018, 2 February). Trump administration dismantles LGBT-friendly policies. *Politico*. www.politico.com/story/2018/02/19/trump-lgbt-rights-discrimination-353774.

Gingrich-Philbrook, C. (2015). On Dorian Street. In Chawla, D. & Holman Jones, S., eds., *Stories of home: Place, identity, exile*, pp. 199–214. Lanham, MD: Lexington Books.

Halberstam, J.J. (1998). *Female masculinity*. Durham, NC and London: Duke University Press.

Halberstam, J.J. (2005). *In a queer time and place: transgender bodies, subcultural lives*. New York: New York University Press.

Haley, J. & Parker, A. (eds.) (2011). *After sex: On writing since queer theory*. Durham, NC: Duke University Press.

Hanisch, C. (1969/2006). *The personal is political.* http://webhome.cs.uvic.ca/~mserra/AttachedFiles/PersonalPolitical.pdf

Hansen, M. (2006). *Bodies in code: Interfaces with digital media.* London: Routledge.

Harris, A. (2014). Ghost-child. In Adams, T.E. & Wyatt, J., eds., *On (Writing) families: Autoethnographies of presence and absence, love and loss.* pp. 69–76. Rotterdam: Sense.

Harris, A. (2016a). Love has a body that feels like heat: (Extra)ordinary affects and genderqueer love. *Departures in Critical Qualitative Research,* 5(4), 24–42.

Harris, A. (2016b). The way we weren't: False nostalgia and imagined love. *Qualitative Inquiry,* 22(10), 779–784.

Harris, A. & Holman Jones, S. (2017). Feeling fear, feeling queer: The peril and potential of queer terror. *Qualitative Inquiry,* 23(7), 561–568.

Hill Collins, P. (2016). Black feminist thought as oppositional knowledge. *Departures in Critical Qualitative Research,* 5(3), 133–144. http://dcqr.ucpress.edu/content/5/3/133.

Holman Jones, S. (2016). Living bodies of thought: The critical in critical autoethnography. *Qualitative Inquiry,* 22(2), 228–237.

Holman Jones, S. (2017). Assembling a we in critical qualitative inquiry. In Denzin, N.K. & Giardina, M.D., eds., *Qualitative inquiry in neoliberal times,* pp. 130–135. New York and London: Routledge.

Holman Jones, S. & Adams, T.E. (2010a). Autoethnography and queer theory: Making possibilities. In Giardina, M. & Denzin, N.K., eds., *Qualitative inquiry and human rights,* pp. 136–157. Walnut Creek, CA: Left Coast Press.

Holman Jones, S. & Adams, T.E. (2010b). Autoethnography is a queer method. In Browne, K. & Nash, C., eds., *Queer methods and methodologies,* pp. 195–214. Burlington VT: Ashgate.

Holman Jones, S. & Harris, A. (2016). Traveling skin: A cartography of the body. *Liminalities (Special Issue: Cartographies: Skins, Surfaces, and Doings): A Journal of Performance Studies,* 12(1), n.p. http://liminalities.net/12-1/.

Holman Jones, S. & Harris, A. (2016). Monsters, desire and the creative queer body. *Continuum,* 30(5), 518–530.

Jung Thapa, S. (2016, 18 November). A global crisis: Epidemic of violence against transgender people. *Human Rights Campaign.* www.hrc.org/blog/a-global-crisis-epidemic-of-violence-against-transgender-people.

Madison, D.S. (2012). *Critical ethnography: Method, ethics, and performance,* 2nd ed. Los Angeles: Sage.

Manovich, L. (2001). *The language of new media.* Cambridge, MA: MIT Press.

Marcus, G.E. & Fischer, M.J. (1999). *Anthropology as cultural critique: An experimental moment in the human sciences.* Chicago: University of Chicago Press.

Massumi, B. (2017). *The principle of unrest: Activist philosophy in the expanded field.* London: Open Humanities Press.

Muñoz, J.E. (2006). Feeling brown, feeling down: Latina affect, the performativity of race, and the depressive position. *Signs,* 31(3), 675–688.

Muñoz, J.E. (2009). *Cruising Utopia: The then and there of queer futurity.* New York: New York University Press.

O'Rourke, M. (2014). *Queer insists.* Brooklyn, NY: Punctum Books.

Pollock, D. (2005). Part I introduction: Performance trouble. In Madison, D.S. & Hamera, J., eds., *The SAGE handbook of performance studies,* pp. 1–8. Thousand Oaks, CA: Sage.

Reed-Danahay, D. (2002). Turning points and textual strategies in ethnographic writing. *Qualitative Studies in Education,* 15(4), 421–425.

Rosaldo, R. (1989). *Culture and truth: The remaking of social analysis*. Boston, MA: Beacon Press.

Ruffalo, D.V. (2016). *Post-queer politics*. New York: Routledge.

Sedgwick, E.K. (1990). *Epistemology of the closet*. Berkeley: University of California Press.

Solnit, R. (2016, 9 June). Why America needs a national rape monument for its countless victims. *The Guardian*. www.theguardian.com/commentisfree/2016/jun/08/america-needs-national-monument-honor-rape-survivors-stanford-case

Spry, T. (2016). *Autoethnography and the other: Unsettling power through utopian performatives*. New York: Routledge.

Stern, D. (1985). *The interpersonal world of the infant*. New York: Basic Books.

Stern, D. (2010). *Forms of vitality: Exploring dynamic experience in psychology, the arts, psychotherapy and development*. Oxford: Oxford University Press.

Stewart, K. (2007). *Ordinary affects*. Durham, NC: Duke University Press.

Sullivan, N. (2003). *A critical introduction to queer theory*. New York: New York University Press.

Taylor, Y. & Snowdon, R. (2014). *Queering religion, religious queers*. New York: Routledge.

Turner, W.B. (2000). *A genealogy of queer theory*. Philadelphia: Temple University Press.

Woolf, V. (1929/2001). *A room of one's own*. Ontario: Broadview Press.

1

QUEERING MONUMENTS

Monument to Rehearsal

We are driving from Melbourne to Alice Springs in a small car packed with books, blankets and a bag or two of groceries—snacks for us and biscuits for Luna, the matriarch cocker spaniel who is dying of cancer.

We are driving the 2,256 kilometers from Melbourne to Alice Springs so that you can do research, so I can see Australia's wide open for the first time, and so Luna can return to her birthplace one last time—a kind of canine 'roots trip' (Harris 2015, p. 162).

We drive the twenty-four hours from Melbourne to Alice Springs in a hurry because Luna is restless in the car—the wincing moan of the steel cattle grates set into the highway makes her unsteady on her feet and unable to sleep.

You drive from Melbourne to Alice Springs while Luna and I sit in the back. She stands, feet planted on either side of my hips, and leans into me. I hold her and hum a song into her ear. Every few kilometers, you reach back and put your hand on Luna's head, resting it there until your arm cramps and you have to move.

When we arrive in Alice, Luna becomes herself again. She sticks her nose out the window and sniffs, pulling the winter desert air into her lungs. You stop the car. I open the door and Luna hops out. She picks her way carefully through the bush, not looking back. She knows we will follow and we do. We walk up and over the crest of a hill, catching sight of Luna just as she lays down on her side in the dry riverbed and kicks her feet.

You say she remembers the geography of this place—the rocks and hills, the scent of the neighborhood you haven't lived in for years, the sound of the river that only flowed a handful of times when you did live there. Memory recollects in her nose and ears, under her feet, in the "pure experience of the welling *now*"

(Manning 2013, p. 73). You say she is walking, running, smelling and swimming as a rehearsal for death.

Performance scholar Theron Schmidt (2015) describes the process of rehearsal as movement that recollects the future. He writes, "we recollect forwards whilst remembering backwards" (p. 5). Rehearsal enacts the "strange temporality" of preparing for an experience in the act of its making. Rehearsal is for making an act that will 'work' in the moment we need it—a play, a dance, a recital, a death. We begin "as if we are looking back at a previous action, a repetition, a re-enactment, even as we look forward to an event that does not yet exist" (Schmidt 2015, p. 5). We rehearse for death as a monument to remembering the welling now of life.

We drive from Melbourne to Alice Springs so that Luna can return to her birthplace and rehearse her death. When we arrive, Luna becomes herself again—emergent, in tune with and attuned to the pulse and scent of her environment, vibrating with the desert taking form beneath her.

> Rehearse—to give an account of.
> To go over again, repeat, literally, to rake over, to turn over.
> From *re*, again and *hercier*, to drag, to trail on the ground.
> To rake, harrow, rip, tear, wound, repeat.
> Rehearse, from *re*, again, and *hearse*—
> a flat framework for candles over a coffin, a large chandelier hung in a church.
> Rehearse, from *re*, again, and hearse, a *harrow*—
> a rustic word containing allusions to wolves' teeth and rakes,
> a means for moving the dead; to wound the feelings, distress.
> To say over again, repeat what has already been said.[1]
> Rehearse—to give an account when
> "what forms us diverges from what lies before us."
>
> *(Butler 2005, p. 136)*

Luna lays down on her side in the dry riverbed and kicks her feet. She is swimming, swimming, swimming in the red dirt water of the Todd Riverbed. The moon rises, illuminating her path, a canopy of ghost gum branches make a harrow for bearing her body.

Monument to Monuments

Monuments mark and remember the passing of time, experiences and beings, though they do so in a present that vibrates with what's yet to come. The monuments we make do not stand in isolation from the culture that brings them into material being but instead as embodiments and enactments of lifeworlds and ways of living. The human act of building cairns or markers to events both culturally grand and personally intimate has been the subject of philosophical investigation for eons (Bradley 2012/1998). In *Placeways: A Theory of the Human Environment*, E.V. Walter articulates a notion of 'topistics,' derived from the Greek word *topos*, as a

> new name by which I hope to renew the context of an old inquiry . . . methods and ideas of a holistic form of inquiry designed to render the identity, character, and experience of a place intelligible. The full range of meaning located as a 'place'—sensory perceptions, moral judgments, passions, feelings, ideas, and orientations—belong to an order of intelligibility that I call 'topistic reality.'
>
> *(1988, p. 21)*

His *topistics* draws on Gaston Bachelard's poetics of space (1958/2014) to "capture poetic features of space . . . a nonfragmentary, theoretical framework to grasp the whole experience of place and space" (1988, p. 18). Walter's theorizing of the 'feelings of place' attempts to incorporate a more holistic intersectioning of "intellect, common sense, and imagination" (1988, p. 21). Here, place is understood as "a location of experience. It evokes and organizes memories, images, feelings, sentiments, meanings and the work of imagination" (1988, p. 21).

Within Walter's somewhat dated articulation lies the seeds of a new materialist understanding of memorials as vibrant matter (Bennett 2009). In this view, monuments are both a material form (or formation) and a "living, vital and immediate" force that has material affects (Nelson & Olin 2003, p. 3). In other words, monuments are *alive*—they have specific ways of being in the world and make themselves felt *as* themselves (Walter 1988, p. 117), just as human bodies are material reminders of other bodies, experiences, memories and sensations.

In this chapter we are concerned with how words build monuments to queer bodies and lives through story (Solnit 2016). Stories stand as memorials to experience, relationally grounding us in particular times and places; stories also *move* us not only emotionally but also in embodied, physical ways. The performance or the *movement* of monuments—how bodies perform and give substance to monuments, how monuments are relational, how monuments create audiences—is an enactment of memory, futurity, politics and love. For queer people, monument making has powerfully served both impulses and needs, perhaps no less powerfully than in the NAMES Project AIDS Memorial Quilt in the US. The 48,000-panel quilt serves as a memorial to the lives of those who have died of AIDS with each 3-foot by 6-foot lovingly stitched by friends, lovers and family members (AIDS Memorial Quilt 2017). The quilt is also a material embodiment of not only the devastating toll of the disease but also the power of a memorial object and its integral role in the movement to raise funds and awareness to battle the AIDS pandemic (AIDS Memorial Quilt 2017).

Storying monuments as movement is what Erin Manning might call "a quasi-virtual experience: actual because all steps actually take place, virtual because all the microperceptions of pastness and futurity are enveloped in the becoming-movement" (2009, p. 38). And as the AIDS Memorial Quilt demonstrates, "the queer storying of monument-as-movement is an act of *willful* remembering—the embodiment of a struggle to exist or transform an existence" (Ahmed 2014, pp. 134, 133). Queer bodies, experiences and lives have often been omitted or forgotten by history and queer people have long fought to combat erasure and neglect. We have fought, too, to mourn of the loss of individual lives alongside the effort to claim and create livable lives as queer people (Butler 2004; see also Crimp 1989; Muñoz 1999; Ahmed 2017).

And what of the monument-body that memorializes?

That struggles to know what to *do* with change, with transformation, and grief, reckoning the body with things passing? That seeks to materialize experience, desire and emotion in an "iterative remembering" (Fitzgerald 2009, p. 86) that is both 'public' and 'personal'?

Garden as Monument

Morning blinks through the gap in the drapes, illuminating the soft swale at the foot of the bed where she slept just yesterday. She is gone, gone, her body carried away—not on a harrow of ghost gum branches—but in my arms. After a walk in sweet grass, a meal befitting a queen and a thousand kisses, we send her off with the whisper of song in her ear. I swaddle her in the blanket that kept her from the cold following our return from the desert and place her in the back seat of the merciful veterinarian's car. We stand in the street, hands in the air, waving her off on her shape-shifting journey.

A week later she returns—body reclaimed by flame to the red dust of her riverbed beginnings. I waver over where she might like best to sit, lie, sleep, make her place in this return to home, but only for a moment. On a sunny Saturday morning, I work her red dirt body into the loamy soil of our garden, the tiny patch of sunshine and natives that was hers and mine. The place we'd go after I'd been away traveling to put our hands and paws into the dirt, to sniff the winter Melbourne air, reanimate to our connection and our bodies. To return to the earth. Ashes to ashes, dust to dust.

Sara Ahmed (2014) writes of "becoming memorial" as a shift from one state or form of relating to another. She writes of becoming memorial in relation to the companionship formed between a man (in this case, the George Eliot character *Silas Marner*) and an earthenware pot that he used to fetch water every day for years. She writes of the sensation and intermingling of touch, body, earth and love:

> Silas is touched by his pot. The pot is his companion; reliable, always lending its handle. . . . The pot is mingled with other things . . . the fresh clear water the pot helps to carry, the body carrying the pot . . . A relation of use is one of affection.

(2014, p. 44)

When the pot, the material object, breaks, the relation of use and our ways of relating shift; what remains is the affection. The broken pot takes up a new use, a new way of relating by "becoming memorial; a holder of memories, not water" (2014, p. 45).

When people and animals and things shift form—through death, in aging, by becoming different in some way or shape or movement—we not only make memorials to what is lost and past, but also *become memorial* in how we reanimate ways of relating and sharing affection. Ahmed connects stories of fragility, breaking, usefulness and affection to queer lives, relationships and politics. She asks us to understand fragility and breaking not as (or only) loss, but rather a "quality of relations we acquire or a quality of what it is we build" (2014, p. 45). Becoming memorial does not make a harrow for bearing or burying companionship, affinities and loves. Rather, it builds a shelter out of story, memory and ghost gum branches.

The space and shift between object-as-memorial and object-becoming-memorial echoes the movement dance scholar Erin Manning (2013) sees in the choreographic potential of material things. A shard of an earthenware pot, a plot of soil, a handful of ashes (and the bodies that encounter them, form relations and attachments to them) becomes more than itself—more than a 'thing' that brings together the "pastness of experience" (the object as we know it) and future worlds and relations (Manning 2013, p. 95; O'Rourke 2014). This movement shows us what bodies and things in relation can do through the very force of taking form and the 'work' they do—including how such movements "stay with us long after the particular occasion of their coming to expression has unraveled" (2013, p. 121). My hands, Luna's ashes and the gum trees that populate our garden make a becoming monument, a place that touches, moves and shifts the very ground that holds us. The garden is a "mobile architecture"—a structure (but not quite) that takes form out of the ash and dust of bone and breath and desert air—to hold a place for Luna and me (Manning 2013, p. 102).

> The garden a place and plot holding memory.
> My hands in the soil, working
> her ashes into the beds we watched over together,
> paying my respects. Memorializing.
> Luna is gone, gone and still—or because of her—
> The garden grows, becoming memorial to
> Touch, to body, to dirt, to love.

Everyday Monuments

> The world
> And the word
> Are monuments
> A life

Is a monument
As strong and true
As stone

I hold place
I stand here
I attest
To something, to animate and intimate others,
People, events, loves, tragedies that have come before me:
I am a monument.

I have thing-ness.
I have substance.
I am here.
This is my body.
I take up space. I comment on my world:
I memorialize.
I attest to liveness, just by being here.
I *am* the monument
To those who have gone before me
I am a *monument.*

I am a performance.
My words and my world are a performance of
Difference
And sameness.
Of liveness and dyingness,
Of here-ness and there-ness.

My life combines the ephemeral with the virtual, the
embodiment of the performance
which itself gestures toward the making of a life-as-monument.
What is the shape of a life?

If you want to build monuments, build them with a voice, a body,
a gesture.
What would my voice monument sound like?
What is a voice?
Why is a voice more ephemeral than a stone?
Here is my voice
There is a stone.

Andy Warhol made artworks from the
Statue of Liberty,
part of his Pop Art series of the 1960s.
Appropriating a timeless icon of America and democratic freedom as
his own,
in 1962 Warhol screenprinted Lady Liberty from an image he found on a
a dimestore postcard ("Andy Warhol in 3D")—in other words, he made
a
small
paper monument
comprised of twenty-four monumental frames.

This is Warhol making a monument to a monument:
"Give me your tired, your poor, your huddled masses yearning to be
famous for about fifteen minutes. . . ."
Why monuments when actions remain unidealistic, unmoved, unchanged,
unfree?

Warhol made the eight-hour film *Empire* on September 11, 1964.
September 11th.
For eight hours, he filmed the Empire State Building in New York
City, looking out the 41st floor of the Time-Life Building in New York
City, from the offices of the Rockefeller Foundation. (Andy Warhol
Empire 1964)

For eight hours, pretty much nothing happens except for the flicker of
floodlights.
The flash of Warhol's face reflected in the window as he switched on the
lights camera to change film reels.
Building, flash. Warhol, window
and back.

Is *Empire* a monument to the unmovable and monumental—stone and
metal?
Or a monument to nothingness, to inertia, to the ordinariness of life?
Or maybe *Empire* is monumental in its everydayness; in its doing and
being.

And maybe—
just when the lights switch off and that everyday is reflected against the
welling darkness—
it is a body becoming. (Manning 2009, p. 6)[2]

Playing Dead in Stone

As 'things,' monuments "share their status with other objects: the term monumentality suggests qualities of inertness, opacity, permanence, remoteness, distance, preciosity, and grandeur" (Nelson & Olin 2003, p. 3). Yet monuments come into being and become important to us personally and publicly "precisely because they are not merely cold, hard, and permanent. They are also living, vital, immediate and accessible, at least to some parts of society" (Nelson & Olin 2003, p 3).

If the body can be monument and the monument is a body, our focus becomes not permanence and remembrance, but performance, negotiation and representation, as both the body and the monument admit to changing "constantly as it renegotiates ideals, status, and entitlement, defining the past to affect the present and future" (Nelson & Olin 2003, p. 7). Monuments as bodies and bodies as monuments challenge the 'subject/object' split, offering us what Donna Haraway (1988) terms 'situated knowledges' created through a partial and situated 'politics of location' (p. 589). Monuments give us a "view from a body, always a complex, contradictory, structuring and structured body," one in contrast with a "view from above, from nowhere, from simplicity" (p. 589).

Performance scholar Peggy Phelan (1997) speaks to the agentic and animate force of situated knowledges in our encounters with the metal and stone of monuments, which in their very solidity and heft "suggest the weight and scope of mourning" (p. 171). Phelan says our rehearsals of grief and efforts to make monuments are motivated by a desire to "forestall and forget death" (Phelan 1997, p. 83). They at once distract us "from the specifics of the dead body and underlin[ing] the stone cold fact of death itself" and remind us that the work of death—and mourning—are never "clear, never complete, never solid" (Phelan 1997, pp. 83, 171). What performance makes manifest is the "drama of corporeality itself," staging how life and death are "at once a consolidated fleshly form and an eroding, decomposing formlessness" (Phelan 1997, p. 3). The desire to "remember and hold bodies" that are gone is a queer desire—both in our efforts to honor the "potent relation to grief" that queer people have (been forced to) experience, as well as our work to write a body becoming monument "toward and against [queer] bodies who die" (Phelan 1997, pp. 154, 4).

Monuments as bodies and bodies as monuments signal the affective relationship of architecture and flesh: "Housed in flesh, we build houses; human form forms the buildings which keep us in them" (Phelan 1997, p. 81). Monuments become 'alive' in relation to other beings; they are bodies becoming events, "mobile architectures" that both "occupy and haunt us, that make it possible to feel the force of incipient form" (Manning 2013, p. 102). Though often what we see in and seek from our monuments is to "cover up a place, to fill in a void: the one left by death" (Hollier 1989, p. 36). We give human form to buildings which we make and find shelter within as a way to forget and forestall death; we play dead in stone so that "death will not come" (Hollier 1989, p. 36). Monuments create a space in which both "death is made to play" and "to be a play" (Phelan 1997, p. 83).

Such 'play' and 'plays' make manifest the "drama of corporeality itself"; we are quite literally staging how life and death are "at once a consolidated fleshly form and an eroding, decomposing formlessness" (Phelan 1997, p. 3). Still, the simultaneous embodiment and erosion of form inherent in performance is, in Phelan's estimation, alive with possibility that "something substantial can be made from the outline left after the body has disappeared"—after the curtain falls; after death. The desire to "remember and hold bodies" that are gone is indeed a queer desire—both in our effort to honor the "potent relation to grief" that queer people have (been forced to) experience, as well as our work to write a body becoming monument "toward and against [queer] bodies who die" (Phelan 1997, pp. 154, 4). This of course includes and remembers the thousands of ill queer bodies claimed by AIDS and murderous homophobic violence. But it also enacts the everyday experience of aging queer bodies as they soften and change but are still no less monuments to the force and heat of life, to a future (still) fueled by desire.

Monument to Readiness Potential

A dream: I am at rehearsal, but I do not know my lines. No, that's not quite right. I'm at rehearsal, but I do not know, cannot say, the *right* lines. It's the kind of play where the character (in this case me, because it's my dream, but it could be you, too) is on stage in a circle of bright light and she's being asked a series of questions by a voice that has no body, a voice that comes from out of the darkness.

The character, my character, is trying to answer the questions based on what she knows, what she thinks the voice thinks she knows, and also what she thinks the voice expects as a right or good answer.

VOICE: What is readiness potential?
CHARACTER: Readiness potential? Okay. Readiness potential: Neurologists describe the electrical movement in the brain that precedes movement of the body and our conscious awareness of the intent to move as 'readiness potential' (Libet 2003).
VOICE: Again, with movement.
CHARACTER: Readiness potential: The term used to describe the interrelationship of voluntary movement and the neurological shift in the electrical activity in the brain that accompanies that movement (Schmidt 2015, p. 5).

In the dream, I'm standing on the stage, offering answers into the darkness which are, it seems to me, right and good, though I'm becoming increasingly nervous, flustered, *warm*. Beads of sweat form on my forehead and under my arms, behind my knees and along the small of my back.

VOICE: Again, with intention.
ME: Readiness potential: the neuro/philosophical construct describing how voluntary movement—the blink of an eye, the turning of a cheek, the

embrace of a lover—is preceded by a movement in the brain, a spark of electricity that accompanies the intention or the decision to move (Schmidt 2015, p. 5).

VOICE: Are we conscious of this?

ME: Of the movement?

VOICE: Of the intention, the decision to move?

ME: We are moved to move—mind and body—and only become conscious of this decision after it has already been made (Schmidt 2015, p. 5).

I become hot, then hotter. I am on fire, but from the inside out. *In fire*.

VOICE: Again, with immanence.

ME: Immanence?

VOICE: Yes.

ME: Readiness potential is what Erin Manning describes as the "immanence of movement moving: how movement can be felt before it actualizes" (2009, p. 6).

VOICE: A kind of affect?

ME: [Nodding]. Yes. We can think of readiness potential as a gathering, a "moment of unformed and unstructured potential," an affective intensity (Shouse 2005, par. 5).

I remove my scarf and sweater and push damp hair out of my eyes. I wonder if I've gotten it; if I have rehearsed the potential of readiness potential. I close my eyes and think about cool things—ice cubes, cantaloupe, winter wind.

VOICE: What is the readiness potential of an aging queer body?

ME: What?

VOICE: What is the readiness potential of a body in desire and decline?

ME: Whose body?

VOICE: Women's bodies. Queer bodies. *Your body*.

ME: Are you asking if I feel the immanence of decay, the spreading heat of desire transforming in my body? In the everydayness and everynightness of. . .

VOICE: Yes. How about if we begin, again, with that. With what you are experiencing. What is the readiness potential of your aging queer body?

ME: Right now?

VOICE: Yes, now. This time, write the readiness potential of your experience.

ME: Writing as a "tangle of created connections," a "compound of created sensations"? (Stewart 2007 p. 4; Deleuze & Guattari 1994, pp. 164–165)

VOICE: [Silence].

ME: Could I. . . .

VOICE: Just begin, please.

ME:

Monument to Ruin

Sudden wave,
autonomic heat.
Blood vessels constricting
body becoming
an empty boat.

Streetlight and cars passing
blink me awake; then the
quick pulse and rush,
body awash in desire.

Pin prick of
something coming apart,
body and mind the rubble
of electricity and matter (Schmidt 2015, p. 5).

Movement taking form in the flash,
memory marching forward
future recollects (Schmidt 2015, p. 9),
disturbing but harmless.

Gathering, more force than form
the immanent, incipient blaze of
the readiness potential of ruin.

VOICE: Thank you. Again, please. What is the readiness potential of an aging queer
    body?

The lights go out. I wake up, sweaty and restless. You stir in the bed next to me.
"It's okay," I say. "Just a hot flash. Go back to sleep."

I throw back the covers and get out of bed. What does it mean to rehearse
something that doesn't yet exist? How can you build a monument to a body that
is gathering the force of a future as it passes?

I find my way in the dark to the kitchen and open the refrigerator. I breathe
in the cool air, eyes adjusting to the light. It has something to do with readiness
potential, with the open and undetermined time and space in which we begin to
make an act that will 'work' in the moment *before* it actualizes. It has something
to do with what Manning (2009) calls preacceleration—"the vital force of movement taking form" (p. 6).

This is the movement of the night sweat—the hot *flash*. In the preaccelera-tion of blood vessel and breath, the concrescence of movement is inseparable from space and time. I am a "body-becoming" (Manning 2009, p. 6)—flushed, heat gathering so forcefully it wakes me up. Out of the dream and into the night.

I let the door of the refrigerator hang open, drinking orange juice from the carton. I tune in to the ways we "come late to our own bodies and are making them, even now, through discovering them" (Schmidt 2015, p. 9). How we notice our decline just when desire becomes delicious, the heat building in the nighttime of our bodies (Jenkins 2005, p. 281; Shaw 2011, p. 71). The hot flash—and with it, memory and desire—becomes not the closing down of experience but instead an opening to queer spacetime[3]—fleeting and compressed and also brimming with the potentiality of a life "unscripted by the conventions of family, inheritance and child rearing" (Halberstam 2011, p. 2). A spacetime for enjoying the fruits of a non-normative life—sweet and perishable, ripe and "rancorously non-reproduc-tive" (Halberstam 2011, p. 101).

Hot flash: to rehearse readiness potential of an aging queer body.
Hot flash: building a monument to a body and a history as if it already exists.

And then, it is over. I move my body backwards and the door of the refrig-erator swings closed, shutting out the light. I walk down the long hallway to the bedroom and slide coolly and quietly under the covers, next to you.

Becoming Monument

Monuments move us in their readiness potential, the vital force of movement tak-ing [a] form that exceeds stone and staging. Becoming monuments are vibrant and experiential—a 'bloc of moment sensation' in Gilles Deleuze and Felix Guattari's sense; "when you experience it you can't quite say where it began or ended, but you can recognize it as a rare example of a work out doing itself" (Manning 2013, p. 102). Manning writes, "It's not the form of the work that stays with you, it's the how of its capacity to dislodge the you that you thought you were. It's the how of the work's capacity to shift the ground that moves you" (2013, p. 102). The force and usefulness of queering autoethnography lives in the how of the story's capac-ity to dislodge to you what you thought you were. The work of queering autoeth-nography outdoes itself in how it shifts our ways of relating to one another. Such stories create mobile architectures—"thought[s] becoming movement[s]"—that reach toward what's possible, though "not-yet" (Manning 2009, p. 101; Muñoz 2009, p. 46) while remaining firmly—willfully—grounded in the need to shelter and memorialize the fragility of queer lives and connections.

Ahmed (2016) describes the concept of willfulness as a process of picking up stones—stones we can carry in our pockets, that we can turn over in our hands, that we can warm with the heat of our bodies, that we can use to build shelter in "places that make it hard to survive" (par. 3–4). And yet, somehow, we find a will do just that—carry, turn over, warm with heat, build shelters and cairns out of stone. "We will, we do" (par. 5). Willfulness as shelter. Stoniness. Willfulness is a "standing against" that minoritarian subjects—women, queers, people of color— embrace in their efforts to both survive and to resist (Ahmed 2014, p. 134, 2016). She writes, "Will is the power not to be compelled by an external force, or by gravity. Will is the power to stop" (Ahmed 2016, par. 12). Willfulness is also a space of potentiality contained within the forces of constraint and denial, a "new beginning, one without blueprint, one in which the capacity to not be compelled by others is made into the promise of a queer thing" (Ahmed 2016, par. 24). Willfulness is a becoming memorial to futurity, a stoniness that holds memories, offers us something to turn over in our hands, and provides us with shelter.

Queer futures depend on the idea of potentialities, rather than possibilities located in the present. José Esteban Muñoz writes,

> Possibilities exist, or more nearly, they exist within a logical real, the possible, which is within the present and is linked to presence. Potentialities are different in that although they are present they do not exist in present things. Thus, potentialities have a temporality that is not in the present, but more nearly, in the horizon, which we can understand as futurity.
>
> *(2009, p. 99)*

They exist as cues—as moments of readiness potential that function "not as a simple tool for the memory of a rehearsed past, but as a call toward the future" (Manning 2013, p. 105). Rather than turn away from an "impoverished and toxic" present for queer people and other non-majoritarian subjects and communities, Muñoz urges us to try and "glimpse another time and place" and build monuments to the "not-yet" (p. 96).

For the Love of Monuments

My life is a monument. Is a life-as-monument.
For proximity
is being alive.
I've loved some monuments in my time.
I've been rebuffed by a few too, oh yes I have.
See, monuments can stand aloof, kind of keep their distance, keep to themselves.
It's hurtful really.
Those hoity-toity monuments.
Fuck you, monuments.

It hurts.
It's all well and good for the general public, sure, but me?

What of the lover?
What of the lovers of monuments?
We get the dregs, we get the shit, we get the tired, hungover, exhausted,
wrung-out, yearning to be free
Washed up monuments.
Everyday monuments.
Queer monuments.

See
my monuments are *words*.
Words in my life are everything: weapons,
wine,
rose petals
tools of seduction, celebration, love, rage,
the written and sonic embodiment of connection. Longing.
Words are my becoming-monuments, the doing of monument.
The climb, leap, roll, tumble, fall, hang, bounce and of course—slam.

Words have material-bodies too; they word-move the air, they word-
punch you in the face
They word-push you from the back
They
lift you up to the word-branch above you, just. Up. *there*.

My slamming words and my fleshbody are virtual monuments in motion
to our
solid stone love.
My stone butch words are a monument to our body-blues and our word-
love and our lasting-ness:
Our words are our bodies are our monuments of love
Let our bodies and words be monuments themselves.
Bodies are monuments of a life lived. And everything passes away.
Everything.

So why do we want our monuments to behave differently than our lives,
our bodies, our own living words?
What do we so fear or find so unsatisfying in this tender aging human
body
that gives and takes and scars and pinches and . . . withers?
That loves and pushes and pulls and weeps and twists and fattens?
Expands and contracts. Expands.
And contracts.

Isn't this a monument to something too? We are breathing monuments to
flesh, to words, to love?
To those functions that the posthuman can't yet do. To the not-yet.[4]

But maybe one day.
When there are fewer of these monuments (pinch yourself)
Maybe one day soon,
when the everlasting metal and stone,
when the unchangeables and unmoveables and unweepables predominate,
when they preside over this tender green and fleshy rotting
planet-monument,
maybe *then* we will see how our bodies were monuments themselves.

Monument to Waking Up

Something happens—an event, an experience, an election—and people begin
saying, begin feeling that they can't work. Or get out of bed. Or wake up from the
bad dream of the "weighted and reeling" present (Stewart 2007, p. 1).

Something surges into view (Stewart 2007, p. 9) and the monument to a new
body (politic) we thought we were building and the history we believed we were
making does not 'work' in the moment we need it. Something happens and suddenly—or so it seems—we are watching the future we were rehearsing, the world
we were recollecting toward, slip away, become lost. Or was it lost—just then?
And if so, to whom? Or what?

Something is lost and people begin feeling, begin asking, just who *are* the people who voted for a present reeling with misogyny, racism, exploitation of workers, disdain for human rights and increased armament and violence? Just who *are*
the people who voted for a future weighed down by neoliberalism, isolationism,
xenophobia?

Something slips and people begin asking: Who are *we*? How did we fail to sense
the preacceleration, the readiness potential of hatred and violence? Have we shielded
ourselves "from the truth by our own isolated form of left and liberal thinking" (Butler
2016)? Have we "believed in human nature in some naïve ways" (Butler 2016)?[5]

Something comes together and people say and feel they can't—work, get out
of bed, wake up from one bad dream and into another. But people do—they
work, they get out of bed, they wake up. They ask, again: what is the readiness
potential of standing up today? Of getting out of bed and rehearsing a world that
'works' in the moment we need it? Deleuze and Guattari (1994) write of the artist's challenge of making a work *work*—of creating something that stands "*up on its
own*," where standing up is "the act by which the compound of created sensations
is preserved in itself—a monument, but one that may be contained in a few marks
or a few lines, like a poem by Emily Dickinson" (pp. 164–165).

Something happens and people begin to ask about, begin to feel the movement moving in the welling *now*, together. In this spacetime, we rehearse our regard for others (Sontag 2003). What does it mean, to rehearse our regard for others? Susan Sontag (2003) argues that "Critics of modernity, consumers of violence as spectacle, adepts of proximity without risk, are schooled to be cynical about the possibility of sincerity. Some people will do anything to keep from being moved" (Sontag 2003, p. 99). And yet to regard—to look, to consider—images of violence and the traumas that give rise to them—is an "invitation to pay attention, to reflect, to learn" (Sontag 2003, pp. 116–117). Accepting that invitation, coming together to look, is how we recognize others and their lives as *grievable* (Butler 2004, p. 20).

We look at something and we return to the "drama of corporeality itself"; becoming audience to a play with and on death in which no action is possible, save that of standing up—like a stone statue, a monument—looking and listening as body after body disappears. In performance, that space of rehearsal of death and desire,

> nothing is required of you but to watch and listen . . . your own inaction is already accounted for . . . the story is not yours and that is why you came here. It is a place to practice—indeed, *to rehearse*—your regard for others.
>
> *(Schmidt 2015, p. 6)*

Something happens and we come together, we look at others and ourselves in all of our precariousness and destruction—and we are moved to be and become differently (Butler 2004, p. 150). To make work that works to recognize and acknowledge ourselves and a world not as it has always been, but to "solicit a becoming, to instigate a transformation, to petition the future always in relation to [each] other" (Butler 2004, p. 44). Returning to soil, ashes, bodies, the queer desire to remember and hold bodies that are gone; to write a body becoming monument one word, one breath, one stone at a time.

> Something happens and we begin, again. We rehearse—
> we say over again, repeat what has already been said, our regard and attachment to others.
> We put our bodies and our words into story, becoming memorials of form giving way to movement; accounts of how "what forms us diverges from what lies before us" (Butler 2005, p. 136).
> We organize. In the now. Again. And again.
> When something or someone is lost, gone—
> And "memory insists she stood there," stands here now,
> "light pulsing through ash" (Forche 1994, p. 55)
> giving way

to something else "unexpectedly hopeful" (Stewart 2007, p. 6).

We build, we are a monument to waking up: one morning, one dream, one work at a time.

Notes

1   Etymological definitions of the words rehearse, hearse and harrow from etymonline. com. "rehearse (v.) . . . 'to give an account of . . . to go over again, repeat,' literally 'to rake over, turn over (soil, ground), from *re-* 'again' . . . + *hercier* to drag, trail (on the ground), be dragged along the ground; rake, harrow (land); rip, tear, wound repeat, rehearse;' from herse 'a harrow' . . . Meaning "to say over again, repeat what has already been said or written" . . . in the sense of "practice a play, part, etc." "hearse (n.), 'flat framework for candles, hung over a coffin' . . . formerly *herce* 'large rake for breaking up soil, harrow'; . . . also 'large chandelier in a church' . . . 'harrow,' a rustic word, from Oscan *hirpus* 'wolf,' supposedly an allusion to its teeth." "harrowing (v.1) . . . 'to drag a harrow over, break or tear with a harrow' . . . In the figurative sense of 'wound the feelings, distress greatly.'"

2   The film takes place between 8:10 pm and 2:30 am on July 25th and 26th, 1964, during which the floodlights on the building come on and flicker, frame by frame, from sunset to sunrise. Each time Warhol and his collaborators Jonas Mekas and John Palmer changed the film reels, they turned on the lights, their faces reflected momentarily in the Time and Life Building windows (Gopnik 2014).

3   In the preface to Erin Manning's (2013) *Always More Than One*, Brian Massumi describes Manning's concept of spacetime as the inseparability of space and time; spacetime brings "seriation and contingency together in the unfolding of the event" (p. xvi). Manning writes that the movement of bodies and the bodying forth of thought— the immanence of movement moving and thought becoming movement—creates the possibility in which "spacetime itself begins to vibrate with movement expression" (p. 101). We are arguing here that menopause might be a spacetime in which bodies become works of art that "exceed their form" and create the "capacity to dislodge the you that you thought you were" (pp. 101–102) and further, that this spacetime is *queer time*—a space that that opens up a "rich and riotous future" out of the structures and strictures of "family time"—the normative time of reproduction (Halberstam 2011, p. 3). In other works, Manning refers to this spacetime. In this book, we have followed the usage as it moves through these works.

4   Muñoz (2009) writes of queer temporality and futurity through Ernest Bloch's notion of the 'not yet here', noting that queer temporalities are "different and outside. They are practiced failure and virtuosic. . . [They insist] on another time and place that is simultaneously not yet here but able to be glimpsed in our horizon" (p. 183).

5   In the wake of the 2016 US presidential election, Judith Butler (2016) writes: "For a world that is increasingly mischaracterized as post-racial and post-feminist, we are now seeing how misogyny and racism overrides judgment and a commitment to democratic and inclusive goals—they are sadistic, resentful and destructive passions driving our country" (par. 3). She continues: "Who are they, these people who voted for him, but who are we, who did not see their power, who did not anticipate this at all, who could not fathom that people would vote for a man with racist and xenophobic discourse, a history of sexual offenses, the exploitation of workers, disdain for the constitution, migrants and a reckless plan for increased militarization? Perhaps we are shielded from the truth by our own isolated form of left and liberal thinking? Or perhaps we believed in human nature in some naive ways. Under what conditions does unleashed hatred and reckless militarization compel the majority vote?" (par. 4).

References

AIDS Memorial Quilt. (2017). www.aidsquilt.org/about/the-aids-memorial-quilt.

Andy Warhol Empire 1964. (2017). www.moma.org/collection/works/89507.

Andy Warhol in 3D. (2017). http://au.phaidon.com/agenda/art/articles/2012/november/12/andy-warhol-in-3-d/.

Ahmed, S. (2014). *Willful subjects*. Durham, NC: Duke University Press.

Ahmed, S. (2016, 29 January). Willful stones. *Feministkilljoys*. https://feministkilljoys.com/2016/01/29/willful-stones/.

Ahmed, S. (2017, 13 January). Queer fatalism. *Feministkilljoys*. https://feministkilljoys.com/2017/01/13/queer-fatalism/.

Bachelard, G. (1958/2014). *The poetics of space*. New York: Penguin.

Bennett, J. (2009). *Vibrant matter: A political ecology of things*. Durham, NC: Duke University Press.

Bradley, R. (2012/1998). *The significance of monuments: On the shaping of human experience in Neolithic and Bronze Age Europe*. London: Routledge.

Butler, J. (2004). *Precarious life: The powers of mourning and violence*. London: Verso.

Butler, J. (2005). *Giving an account of oneself*. New York: Fordham University Press.

Butler, J. (2016). *A statement from Judith Butler*. http://conversations.e-flux.com/t/a-statement-from-judith-butler/5215?u=anton.

Crimp, D. (1989). Mourning and militancy. *October*, 51, 3–18.

Deleuze, J. & Guattari, F. (1994). *What is philosophy*. Trans. G. Burchell & H. Thomlinson. London: Verso.

Fitzgerald, E.M. (2009). Commemoration and the performance of Irish famine memory. In Brady, S. & Walsh, F., eds., *Crossroads: Performance Studies and Irish culture*, pp. 86–99. London: Palgrave Macmillan.

Forche, C. (1994). *The angel of history*. New York: Harper Collins.

Gopnik, B. (2014, 16 January). Monumental cast, but not much plot: Andy Warhol's 'Empire' shown in its entirety. *The New York Times*. www.nytimes.com/2014/01/17/arts/design/andy-warhols-empire-shown-in-its-entirety.html.

Halberstam, J. (2011). *The queer art of failure*. Durham, NC: Duke University Press.

Haraway, D. (1988). Situated knowledges: The science question in feminism and the privilege of partial perspective. *Feminist Studies*, 4, 575–599.

Harris, A. (2015). A kind of hush: Adoptee diasporas and the impossibility of home. In Chawla, D. & Holman Jones, S., eds., *Storying home: Place, identity, and exile*, pp. 161–175. New York: Lexington Books.

Hollier, D. (1989). *Against architecture: The writings of George Bataille*. Trans. B. Wing. Cambridge and London: The MIT Press.

Jenkins, M.M. (2005). Menopause & desire or 452 positions on love. *Text and Performance Quarterly*, 25(3), 254–281.

Libet, B. (2003). Can conscious experience affect brain activity? *Journal of Consciousness Studies*, 12(12), 24–28.

Manning, E. (2009). *Relationscapes: Movement, art, philosophy*. Cambridge, MA: MIT Press.

Manning, E. (2013). *Always more than one: Individuation's dance*. Durham, NC: Duke University Press.

Muñoz, J.E. (2009). *Cruising utopia: The then and there of queer futurity*. New York: New York University Press.

———. (1999). *Disidentifications: Queers of color and the performance of politics*. Minneapolis: University of Minnesota Press.

Nelson, R.S. & Olin, M. (2003). *Monuments and memory, made and unmade*. Chicago and London: University of Chicago Press.

O'Rourke, M. (2014). *Queer insists* (for José Esteban Muñoz). Brooklyn: Punctum Books.

Phelan, P. (1997). *Mourning sex: Performing public memories*. London: Routledge.

Rehearse, hearse, harrow. (2016). www.etymonline.com.

Schmidt, T. (2015). Some people will do anything to keep themselves from being moved. *Performance Research*, 20(5), 4–9.

Shaw, Peggy. (2011). *A menopausal gentleman: The solo performances of Peggy Shaw*. Ann Arbor: University of Michigan Press.

Shouse, E. (2005). Feeling, emotion, affect. *M/C Journal*, 5, 8. http://journal.media-culture. org.au/0512/03-shouse.php.

Solnit, R. (2016, 15 July). 'Hope is an embrace of the unknown': Rebecca Solnit on living in dark times. *The Guardian*. www.theguardian.com/books/2016/jul/15/ rebecca-solnit-hope-in-the-dark-new-essay-embrace-unknown.

Sontag, S. (2003). *Regarding the pain of others*. New York: St. Martins.

Stewart, K. (2007). *Ordinary affects*. Durham, NC: Duke University Press.

Walter, E.V. (1988). *Placeways: A theory of the human environment*. Chapel Hill and London: University of North Carolina Press.

2

QUEERING MASSACRES

Facing Precarity

Sometimes I joke that my life has been a queer massacre, though not in the large and encompassing sense of the term; rather in the wearing down of hundreds of tiny massacres. Though sometimes this life feels like a queer victory as well. The truth is, my life has been queered in more ways than sexuality, and I have experienced exclusion and harm along my multiple axes for as long as I can remember. Yet queer has also given me a generative and expansive lens through which to see the ubiquity of injustice in this world. Marching against state-sanctioned violence is now almost a full-time job. Between sticking up for ourselves and being allies to others, we are almost out of time, or just getting by.

It's true that death-making policies at the government, collective and familial level all hurt. It's true that these socially sanctioned violations are at least more transparent than they have ever been before. Perhaps that's because I've lived long enough to see change, backsliding and more change happen again and again. There is a special kind of exhaustion that comes with having been around this block before. To see not only 'oppression' in the general sense continue, but also oppression in the exact same formats and enactments, can be soul-destroying. We need more than protest. We need a deeper awareness of the intersectionality of all oppressions, and how these compounded abuses are threatening the planet in not just abstract but large-scale material ways. Queering massacres is about these interconnections, and like all autoethnography, queer or not, this commentary is grounded in our own senses of intersectional grief, anger and compounded harms. It also has roots in our deep knowledge that the only way forward is *through*, and that involves looking to ourselves to heal the harms we continue to perpetrate against ourselves and others. So this writing is not about our queerness or queer subjectivities in and of themselves. Instead, it's about the precarity of minoritarian lives in massacre culture and where it might lead us if we do not wake up while there's still time.

We draw on four types of 'massacres' as examples of how the queerness of massacre culture cuts across communities of difference and shares a politics of activism against death-making and the vanishing of non-white, non-straight and non-male bodies. The first considers the "slow death" of everyday structural violations based on difference, the second *appears* to be related to queer people at the intersections of race and religion,[1] the third to life in the quest for economic domination in the name of an American dream, and the last takes life from the planet and other sentient beings. We argue that we are living in a 'massacre culture,' a state in which any known sense of safety has disappeared, despite the material interventions available to us. In a word, we are living a precarious existence. We use precarity in Butler's (2006) sense, as "an acknowledgment of dependency, needs, exposure and vulnerability" (Puar 2012, p. 163). Butler's (2006) development of the relational nature of precarity draws from Emmanuel Levinas's (1996) notion of "face," which she takes to mean "that for which no words really work; the face seems to be a kind of sound, the sound of language evacuating its sense" (p. 134). To respond to the face, to the sound, to the affective force of that which precedes sense, understanding and movement means to

> be awake to what is precarious in another life, or rather, the precariousness of life itself. This cannot be an awakeness . . . to my own life, and then an extrapolation from an understanding of my own precariousness to an understanding of another's precarious life. It has to be an understanding of the precariousness of the Other.
>
> *(Butler 2006, p. 143)*

A relational and ethical understanding of precarity, Levinas writes, happens in the "face of the other in its precariousness and defenselessness. . . [and is] at once the temptation to kill and the call to peace in the admonition 'You shall not kill'" (Levinas 1996, p. 167). Of the invocation of the commandment, 'Thou shall not kill,' Butler writes:

> Why would it be that the very precariousness of the Other would produce for me a temptation to kill? Or why would it produce the temptation to kill at the same time that it delivers a demand for peace? . . . [The] face makes various utterances at once: it bespeaks an agony, an injurability, at the same time it bespeaks a divine prohibition against killing.
>
> *(2006, p. 135)*

The precarity or impossibility of safety in massacre culture means that citizens exist in a constant state of hypervigilance and carry an embodied and affective sense of injurability. The anxiety that massacre culture produces at ever-alarming rates can swamp interpersonal and cultural connection, as well as peace, in a culture that seems to perpetuate massacre in even the most mundane ways.

The Slow Death of Everything You Want

What does it mean to queer the kinds of massacres that have become everyday occurrences? Autoethnography offers productive interventions into the dehumanization of massacres in the media. Queer theory offers similar opportunities for holding a new lens up to the business-as-usual of scholarly research and dominant discourses and practices. In an age when massacres are part of our every day, both autoethnography and queer theory can be used to refuse the banality narrative of 'just another massacre' that the mainstream media and corporate/political structures ask us to take for granted. As women, as queers, as artists, as activists, as scholars and as citizens, we refuse to remain unmoved by the systematic loss of human and other life, despite (and because of) its ubiquity across the landscapes of our lives. We recognize that for our own sakes and that of the earth, the animals and all other sentient beings with which we cohabit, we must *see* these recurring massacres as unacceptable and that seeing, in its very necessity, must be queer in the sense of the interruption and disruption of queering practices (Ahmed 2006).

As a way into and through this kind of sight, we want to create some "dissonance around what passes as normal" (Holman Jones 2016) by telling this story as it "moves between selves/structures," relying on the split and disjuncture between these voices and discourses, and the institutional, emotional and embodied differences they draw to underline the need—and the possibility of "projecting in turn alternative figures of social relation" (Pollock 1998, p. 87).

I was being "urged" (bullied?) into taking on a major role at my new institution. A role in addition to the one I'd been hired for. A role without compensation—material or otherwise—attached to it. For the first three months of my appointment I tried to negotiate—fairly but assiduously—for compensation attuned to what I thought the role required, for what I thought I deserved. My request and argument was simple: I was asking for, and should be provided, compensation equal to that which others with the same level of responsibility were already receiving. I was told by several colleagues in many meetings the role would improve my profile and the profile of the institution. That I was too new to ask for compensation. That I should take on the role, prove myself, and then ask for compensation as recognition and reward.

There are also what we call mundane annihilations, the everyday degradations associated with making minoritarian positions, persons and practices visible. The making-visible of queer and other minoritarian subjects in contemporary cultures of terror equals a kind of everyday or mundane annihilation, in which non-dominant subjects not only fear for a backlash against difference (going far beyond the panopticon metaphor of surveillance and even sousveillance), we expect it.

We see it all around us every day. We live nonconforming lives in Lauren Berlant's (2007) sense of the "slow death" of precarity, "socialized into the intensification of the ordinary work of living" (p. 761).

After three months of these kinds of meetings, on the eve of the announcement of my assumption of the role—crafted without resolution of the "compensation conversation" in—what? the hopeful event that I would accept the empty hand they were offering, I finally became angry. I turned to the two senior scholars—a male dean and a well-known female research scholar— invited to the latest meeting with the university administrator, and said: "Why should I do it? You wouldn't come in the door of this place if you weren't adequately compensated for what they ask you to do."

The research scholar, obviously startled by both my anger and my directness, looked at me. She paused for several moments and then said, "Why must you fight? You don't need to fight like this! Just stop fighting. You have arrived. You have everything you want."

The senior research scholar was urging me to do what she herself would not do—was not doing. In fact, she had just resigned from this role, which precipitated the negotiations. When I attempted to fight for myself by demanding that I wanted—which by the way is the advice I'd been given for years under the heading "'women' don't" get the same promotions or opportunities as 'men' in the academy because they don't demand them"—I was viewed as both combative and overemotional. I wondered, would they have asked a male-presenting colleague to do a senior leadership role for free?

What role did my queerness, my perceived (or not perceived) gender play in those negotiations? We can't know, but we can know that the injunction to stop fighting is a mundane annihilation.

As Berlant writes: Slow death is not a state of exception to the change and crisis of "catastrophe" or "mere banality," but a "domain of revelation where an upsetting scene of living that has been muffled in ordinary consciousness is revealed to be interwoven with ordinary life after all, like ants revealed scurrying under a thoughtlessly lifted rock" (p. 762). As visibly different, we measure the violence of our lives not on 'what-if,' or 'what's worse' scales, but rather the everyday- or micro-annihilations of having, it seems, to always fight.

The slow death of mundane annihilation is contained in the response, "You don't need to fight . . . Just stop fighting," because the distress of queer people and other minoritarian people is not seen as crisis and catastrophe, but rather as a "problem the world can live with" (p. 762).

It's a slow death by the "structural intractability of a problem the world can live with" (Berlant 2007, p. 762). It is an everyday assault, and the accumulation of mundane annihilations is what begins to erode communities of differences both within and without.

Mundane annihilations are the 'micro-aggressions' that serve as reminders that we are precarious, the 'suggestion' that we are on the 'inside' only at the discretion of the insiders. They begin in families and they are mirrored in the larger culture (Harris et al. 2017; Schulman 2016, 2009).

Mundane annihilations accumulate to remind us that whether it is happening to us (yet) or not, we live in an age of queer terror (Harris & Holman Jones 2017) and that precarity takes its toll.	. . . we live in an age of queer terror (Harris & Holman Jones 2017) and that precarity takes its toll.

An Astonishment Very Close to Fear[2]

Massacre culture is the constant state of fear in which minoritarian subjects respond with/to traumatic events whether they happened to us or not, because we know that in these times of terror it is better to be prepared than to not be. So what does it mean to live in a massacre culture in which queers and other minoritarian subjects see systematic violence again others who are precarious (whether they are 'us' or 'not us,' the message feels, and indeed might be, the same). We understand that it might (or will) be us. Like mundane annihilations, massacre culture is an accumulation of trauma, experienced or observed, that everyone living under massacre culture feels but that some of us experience as a matter of our every day.

The effects of this are also sometimes cumulatively and sometimes violently felt when we come together—when we assemble ourselves to shake off the mundane annihilations to punctuate our everyday in company and concert. Say at a meeting in a so-called safe space—a café or a bar. Or a dance club, dimly lit, "an undulating mass of bodies . . . spread wall to wall"; the kind of assemblage that gives rise to "a kind of heart-thudding astonishment," an acknowledgment and recognition that we are, indeed, part of a community (Delaney 1988, p. 173). That astonishment, though, as William Delaney's shimmering description of his first visit to the St. Marks bathhouse in 1963 powerfully reminds, is "very close to fear."[3]

In her recent work, Judith Butler (2015) elaborates on what happens when we come together, body to body, in a public space. She asserts that when we gather our bodies in space, we assemble a 'we' that performatively enacts a claim to the political (Holman Jones 2017, p. 130). When we come together, we become, in effect "the social plurality" we seek (Butler 2015, p. 175). Whether we're in the public square, in a bathhouse or on the dance floor in an Orlando nightclub, when we come together, we become 'we the people' and our undulating bodies are "already speaking before [they] utter any words" (p. 156).

Back in the day Back in the day of coming out Of 'what is AIDS?' Of sweet innocence and queer rage	Butler (2015) says that public assembly speaks—materially, emotionally and intellectually a "relation of freedom," one made through a mutual relation and

Back in that day bars used to be the place we'd go to find community.

Bars—and bathhouses and cafés—were safe places in cities like New York and lines were crossed between genders and sexualities and there was policing sure but there was also fluidity and understanding that what one *said* one is, is what one is. Or rather, what one does. What one wants.

That gender or sexuality or any sense of the self is, in the end, only what one *has*.[4] So one sought out these places of *sanctuary*.

These gathering places were our safety. Or at least we believed it was so, and that belief gave us comfort and we could exhale.

We believed we could walk up Christopher Street to Sheridan Square and drop in on roomfuls of women, men and trans★ people and share a cool drink or play pool, the "green baize like moss."[5]

Believed we could lean our heads together and speak without being careful what we say. Believed we could dance "under twirling silver moons that rain light down in glittering drops."[6]

These days, bathhouses and bars and places of worship—anything particularly queer, particularly Muslim, particularly female, particularly queer—these days it's frightening to gather in such places. To speak or drink or pray together. To dance by twos under silver moons or in large groups to the pulse of bass and light.

need (pp. 88, 179). Speaking a relation of freedom can be "showing up, standing, breathing, moving, standing still, speech and silence" (p. 18). Dancing. Any of these "unpredictable and transitory" gatherings can put "livable life at the forefront of politics" (p. 18). Can create a space for asserting both community and the right to assemble and to live without fear. Though can we gather, today, without queer terror?

We have argued that the notion of *queer terror* (Harris & Holman Jones 2017) is an affective condition not limited to queer or other minoritarian subjects, and that its relationship to fear, hate, factionalism and isolationism is a central component of the growing consciousness of terrorism as an affective state, not action. *Queer terror* is both an enactment of terror against queer subjects and a queering of massacre culture itself. Does queer terror, through the act and its viral media representations, create minoritarian public spheres that can be shared by queer people of color (QPOC) and allies alike? Does affective queer allyship seek community both in response to—and as a refusal of—the kinds of terror that made the shooting in Orlando's Pulse nightclub possible?

The massacre at the Pulse nightclub in Orlando, Florida, in June 2016 was the deadliest mass shooting and the deadliest incident of violence against LGBT people in the US since the September 11 attacks in 2001, claiming the lives of 49 and wounding 53 people. The massacre was decried as a targeted attack on the Latino LGBT community, though media coverage focused on the shooter's possible links to terrorist organizations.

These days, it's better not to gather at all, or if we do, to assemble ourselves in bits and pieces, then disperse. It's becoming more and more difficult to feel strength in numbers that isn't overwhelmed by fear—of exposure, vulnerability. Of catastrophe.

We find solidarity in gathering, in coming together to speak our outrage and fear, but is it? Solidarity? When we march, even when we like something on social media, we look over our shoulders because we are all pretty sure now that we are being watched, tagged, tracked and gathered. They know where we are and if they want to find us, they will. Where is the sanctuary, the freedom of assembly, the feeling of safety in numbers, now?

Still, we persist. Assemble ourselves in relation to one another. Gather together. We put ourselves in contact out of interdependency and a desire to feel welcome, solidarity, touch. Out of need.

We make queer spaces in our everyday, as a means of combating the slow death and mundane annihilations of office politics, familial homophobia, queer fatigue in the ongoing battle to secure even the most basic protections and rights, "forms of catastrophe [the] world is comfortable with or even interested in perpetuating."[7]

We make those spaces looking into each other's eyes on trains and embracing in hallways.

We make those spaces in twitter feeds and likes and swiping right.

Queer terror is what happens in times and positions of precarity—moments and circumstances and gatherings that expose "our sociality, the fragile and necessary dimensions of our interdependency" (Butler 2015, p. 119).

Queer terror is shot through with the "apocalypticism" of contemporary life, captivated as we are with the possibility of "imminent catastrophe" that creates a near-constant state of unease and fear (Stewart & Harding 1999, p. 286). Such unease and fear depends, as Butler points out, on an unequal distribution of risk and vulnerability governed by "dominant norms regarding whose life is grievable and worth protecting and whose life is ungrievable, or marginally or episodically grievable, and so, in that sense already lost in part or in whole and thus less worthy of protection and sustenance" (Butler 2015, p. 119).

And still, we persist. Assemble ourselves. Gather. And we wonder if in that gathering we *queer* the everydayness of queer terror. Drawing on Muñoz's "depressive position" as a flash point for minoritarian aesthetics and political practices, which he articulates through "feeling down, feeling brown," we see queer terror at work in how we both "feel queer" and "feel fear" as queer subjects searching for "affective particularity" and belonging in an age of fear and terror (2006, p. 563). It is a "position we live in" both in the world and our understandings of what safe spaces might be available to us, and with that understanding, ourselves (Muñoz 2006, p. 681).

Just as Muñoz's theorizing shifts constructions of race and ethnicity from identity constructions—who or

We make those spaces in poetry written as a "door that opens into a room where [we] want to go."[8] In flashes to story brilliant and vibrant as strobe lights in the dark, the dance shown as rapture, head thrown back in astonishment.[9]

And still, we make those spaces in the familiar gathering places of the bathhouse, the bar, the café, the church.

We make those spaces in the dance club.

We make those spaces to speak, invoke and actualize a 'we' that names needs, desires and demands not yet fully known, and whose coming together is bound up in a future that is yet to be lived.[10]

"Queerly beloved, we are gathered here today to get through this thing,"[11] to assemble our story, "stretched across bloodlines, backrooms and borderlines."[12]

An act of persistence.

A need to gather together and "remember, honor, dance through our worst fears,"[13]

In the places that have given us sanctuary.

Spaces that have given us a livable life and a certain kind of hope.

what someone is—to the affective and performative "feeling" and "doing" of subjectivities—what someone has and does—so too were the people gathered in the nightclub "feeling" and "doing" queer—whether they were same-sex attracted, gender nonconforming, Latino, or not. In their very assembly, the people in Pulse experienced terror in a queer chain of connection and recognition (Munoz, p. 687).

Muñoz describes this chain of recognition as a circuit of "affective particularity" that is collectively performed and deployed by minoritarian subjects and that contains within it a potentiality of working through, reparation and a "certain kind of hope" (p. 687). It is a doing that is not only or simply a "breakdown of the self or the social fabric," a giving in to grief, loss and despair, but that also creates a position from which to negotiate history and reality and attentiveness to the self in an effort to know the other (p. 687). In this sense, the *queering* of queer terror might ultimately be a queering of public gathering (Harris & Holman Jones 2017) that refuses the kinds of terror that make what happened in the Pulse nightclub possible. And maybe, in that queering, we can find the sanctuary in which to enact the kind of relational freedom that puts creating a "livable life at the forefront of politics" (Butler 2015, p. 18).

The Frame of Injurability

In order for a life to be grievable, it must be socially and historically intelligible to bystanders, consumers, co-constitutive others (Butler 2009, p. 6). However, in order to be intelligible, a life must conform to "certain concepts of what life is . . . so that we can and do have histories of life and histories of death" (p. 6). Those histories—of life and of death—depend on what counts as living and what counts as life (p. 8). And we know that while some of us may indeed be apprehended or understood as "living," we exist outside the norms of life. Become problems to be managed. Fall outside the frame of who and what counts.

A truck used for human trafficking crossed the Mexican-American border, parked in a Walmart parking lot in San Antonio, Texas, in the middle of summer, and the 60-year-old driver from Florida fled, failing to seek help even after he became aware of at least one fatality in the back of his truck. This border-crossing massacre claimed 10 lives outright, but another 90+ lives were devastated in the heat-and-suffocation chamber before they were found. This heartbreaking scene of such disregard for human life certainly evokes what Judith Butler has called the distinction between "grievable lives" (2009) and ungrievable ones.

We grieve the death-making of that truck, that driver, that parking lot in the blistering Texas heat, the invisible devastation, even when discovered, contained and wrought in the work of human trafficking. We grieve too the knowledge that this event, in no way singular in the movements of human trafficking, is equally unremarkable in a long history of dehumanizing practices of migrants, refugees and those suffering under the weight of capitalism, racism, religious persecution, homo- and trans*phobia, stigmas attached to differences in mental and physical abilities, and other manifestations of difference.

It is not incidental that it occurred (or was finally 'seen') in the parking lot of a Walmart, a well-known corporate symbol of capitalist greed and disregard for small business and a living wage. There's symbolic cruelty in the lack of media coverage of this event, and the unwillingness to typify it as a 'terrorist' act, almost always required to be perpetrated by a non-white, non-American or non-western/global northern citizen. The event and this lack of attention are evidence that massacre culture permeates.

Such little media coverage of the truck and the trafficking and the devastation of human lives deemed undeserving of protection and persistence, let alone flourishing, compared to how much an unsuccessful or unevidenced 'terrorist' attack receives. We recognize the influence on this event of a cultural, political and physical pattern of vilification. We recognize, too, the links between this event and the privileges of writing as a means and method of making precariousness and death known. Of making the value of life intelligible in the context and history of those lives. In other words, the privileges of writing a life that matters. A life that is grievable.

The social and political networks in which we live must regard and treat these lives as worth living, worth preserving and worth mourning (p. 53). In the case of the truckload of Mexican hopefuls coming into Texas, the horror of the event is not diminished but exaggerated by the inability of many Americans to feel empathy for the victims. This massacre pivots on a cultural narrative which believes that all 'decent' Americans can 'make it' if they work hard enough; at the same time it plays

We recognize that we have time to reflect, to write, to share our stories in spaces where we can be seen, felt and heard. We have the access and ability to make queer spaces in which to gather, to speak and to find recognition in the face of an other. Even in writing moments of risk, loss, vulnerability and un/intelligibility we recognize how we are able to construct stories in the hope, if not knowledge, that we are worthy of care. That because of the time and space to reflect and write and share these stories, our lives are grievable.

out what the fear of outsiders who are trying to somehow contaminate the 'American' way of life can do. Does. Indeed, by fall, popular discourse had turned to Trump's repeal of President Obama's Deferred Action for Childhood Arrivals (DACA), which protects people brought into the US as children from deportation and allows them to work and receive insurance benefits, but not a path to citizenship (Dickerson 2018). Newspapers and news channels were filled with earnest defenses and condemnations of 'The Dreamers.' Yet no media outlets seemed to connect these victims of the dream with the Dreamers at risk in Trump's policy reform.

This is one event in a long tradition of bias-related violations. As Aho et al. (2017) remind us, all such events are "connected to much longer histories of racialization, affectivity and disablement, but their coalescence in this violent instance of racialized, able-nationalist arrangements of power speaks to the importance of thinking about the co-constitution of race and disability in the *longue duree* of racial capitalism and liberal modernity" (p 291).

It is a violation that trades on and exploits the precariousness of those who are made vulnerable in these arrangements of power; their lives, as Butler (2009) notes, are "in the hands of the other," which "implies exposure to those we know and to those we do not know; a dependency on people we know, or barely know, or know not at all" (p. 14). In that unknowing and exposure, the massacre discovered in the Walmart parking lot began long before the corporation or the driver or the truck or hopeful people pressed into that deadly space.

We acknowledge, too, that in and because of the privilege to write, we have an ethical responsibility to lay bare the ways that race, gender and class determine whose stories (and bodies) matter in that writing.

We write and read about lives lived and lost in a culture of massacre and mundane annihilations, giving the numbers and the demographics and times and places and the movements of death-making (immediate or slow). We read and recount messages of terror and farewell sent from underneath desks or bathroom floors and we imagine those unsent from bomb sites or the back of a suffocating tractor-trailer.

We read and we write, though the stories about lives lived and lost are "repeated every day, and the repetition appears endless, irremediable. And so, we have to ask, what would it take not only to apprehend the precarious character of lives lost . . . but to have that apprehension coincide with an ethical and political opposition to the losses" these massacres entail? (Butler 2009, p. 13). We have to ask about the conditions under which it becomes possible to write about a life or set of lives as precarious and those under which it becomes impossible to do so.

Writing within this frame of privilege, we have to ask about the precariousness of the frame of massacre. To frame, in our writing, the frame of injurability that the truck in Texas can never quite contain and how what happened exceeds the frames that trouble our sense of reality.[14]

Toxic Animacies

Massacre culture doesn't confine itself to the human. We live in an age of rolling environmental massacres and the questions about vulnerable, injurable, grievable bodies are in some ways more difficult to ask amidst the repetition of endless, irremediable annihilations. Consider, for example, two recent examples of oil drilling and spilling as environmental massacre culture: the battle over the proposed Dakota Access Pipeline at Standing Rock, North Dakota, and the Deepwater Horizon oil spill in the Gulf of Mexico. In addition to the cost of these violations—human, ecological, economic, sociopolitical and more—the disaster and displacement of these events are felt in the welling and ongoing movements of what Mel Y. Chen (2012) calls "disaster migrants" (p. 226), those displaced by the oil spill/s—both human and nonhuman. Chen and other new materialists argue that instantiations of vibrancy and animacies of the nonhuman are not 'inert'; here we also attend to the 'dead,' the culturally cast off, the antithesis of lives that matter. In massacre culture, these are the lives that don't matter, that aren't seen, that don't get counted, that aren't remembered (Hyner & Sterns 2009).

In December 2016, the largest gathering of Indigenous nations in modern American History joined the Standing Rock Sioux tribe to protest the construction of the 1,172-mile-long Dakota Access Pipeline, which cuts across the Dakotas, through Iowa and into Illinois.

The proposed $3.8 million construction project began in June 2016, but was disrupted for four months from September to December when thousands of protesters defended themselves from tear gas, concussion grenades, water cannons and rubber bullets (Gambino 2017). Construction was halted by an Obama administration order denying an easement to sacred land, but in February 2017, Donald Trump signed an executive order overturning it (Visser 2017). The protesters were evicted from the site and construction resumed (Dakota Access Pipeline 2018). The pipeline was completed in April 2017; even before it became fully operational in May, 84 gallons of crude escaped at a South

I have a habit of sticking precious or problematic keepsakes into books. They live on my shelves, they hold my secrets and they are like old friends. On occasion they reappear and with them a long-forgotten story, or moment, or intensity is unearthed. Unleashed. So it was the other night. We'd recently moved to a new house and I was going through my books as I replaced them on new bookshelves. A white business-size envelope and old-fashioned handwritten address popped out of a novel. The postmark is February 9, 1996. The letter, the handwriting, the envelope, the stamp smeared with the postmark stop me dead in my tracks. I am struck by the power of words, of paper to stop and start time. To stop and start injury.

I had in fact forgotten about it, this letter. I only ever remember receiving one letter from my birthmother, Dorothy Barnowski, the single page on which she tells me my blood type and then

Dakota pump station (Grenoble 2017).[15] The reverberations of the construction of the pipeline, the protest, the stay, the overruling order and the spill signal the reach and uncertainty of massacre culture. "This leak hits close to home, my home," said Joye Braun of the Cheyenne River Sioux, "Do we have more spills just waiting to happen?" (qtd. in Grenoble 2017). Part of the precarity of massacre culture is the ever-present sense that nothing is reliable; no safety feels complete or permanent. Things are temporary and vulnerable to change and in this flux, one can never rest.

In the afterword to *Animacies*, Chen does a powerful posthuman riff on the 2010 Deepwater Horizon oil spill in the Gulf of Mexico, which ruptured and went unabated for five long months, spilling an estimated two hundred million barrels of oil into waters of the Gulf (p. 233). Chen dives underneath and beyond the nearly unfathomable loss of planet life and health from this human 'accident' to take us into life-and-death "animation of the oil" which included how "some of it evaporated, and some of it settled, and some of it got consumed by the 'naturally occurring' bacteria in the Gulf" (p. 225). They write, "At bottom, [the] toxic spill was a *lifely* thing, lifely, perhaps beyond its proper bounds. The well itself was alive, and not only because something had flowed out of it with such vivid animation. It was a threat *to* life in the Gulf, as well as a *way* of life" (p. 227). Here the frame—the "overbearing use of dead and killed"—work as a framing of the frame of injurability as animating and animate.

Chen considers the categories of "animality, sexuality, race, ability" in regard to one another, and offers the notion of animality as a mediating and interruptive move which can also be considered queer for its disruptive power, "in light of queer's own mutative animacy," as "a way to think about queer animality as a genre of queer animacy,

tells me to fuck off. So when I started reading this one—the previously forgotten and newly found letter—I realized that I'd mixed things up. I realized that there were, indeed, two letters from my mother. And I remembered—because I have always known this, that outside of that letter—those two letters, I've had no contact with Dorothy for over 20 years. Not a word, though I've been waiting for something to happen all my life.

I knew the letter would be hard to read, so I put it on my bedside table and waited. Two days later, when we were going to bed and I was feeling pretty good overall, I got up the nerve to read it out loud. The sweep of her handwriting blurs in my vision.

You want to proceed and I don't.
You refuse to accept my responses.
Just because you found me doesn't mean you can have me.
I do not want to be your friend nor do I want to be your mother.

I can only see the underlined words: want, accept, found, friend, mother. But I feel the loss of their surround. Her words, those five pages of handwritten text—is a lifely thing—and surely beyond its proper bounds. The letter itself was alive, and not only because something—anger, refusal, recrimination—had flowed out of it with such vivid animation. It was a threat to my life, as well as a way of life of belonging. The overbearing use of "do not" and "will not" frame the frame in injurability as animating and animate.

My adoptive mother Anna Mae died in 2007. At the end of her life, she was not only suffering physically, but she was as a modulation of life force" (p. 98). In other words, Chen considers how animacy itself can be queer in how it blurs the tenuous human–nonhuman hierarchies with which it is associated (p. 98).

What does it mean to reconsider the hierarchy of value of life on this planet? What does it mean to consider apprehension and recognition of both human and nonhuman *lifely* things, threats to life and ways of life as mutually constitutive, intersectional and inseparable?

The non-creatures that Chen writes about in *Animacies* include the molecules and chemicals that permeate our everyday lives. Chen's argument for the sentience or aliveness of things is explained in terms or language and the work of nouns. To illustrate, they use the fragment, "The hikers that rocks crush," inverting the agentic subject of the sentence from the hiker to the rock. Chen extends this argument into a discussion of privilege and status, linking our hierarchies of 'aliveness' with the valuing and marginalization of subjects based on a naturalized logic where the white male is at the top, and where people of color, and all minorities, including slaves and women as objects, people with disabilities are "vegetables," and others are on the bottom of the animacy hierarchy (pp. 233, 41).

To underline the mutuality of this hierarchy, Chen shows how toxic metals, such as lead and mercury, not only gain animacy through their toxic connotations, but also how racial hierarchies are created around the treatment of these toxic metals. Take, for example, the 2007 'lead panic' in the United States, during which fear and suspicion circulated around Chinese-manufactured products (p. 160). During this panic, lead—an inanimate metal—became racially animated through representations of China as a threat to United States livelihood and as a country terrorizing American babies with poison toys.[16]

withdrawn, angry and bitter. She had suffered mental health problems for several years, on medication for depression, suicidal tendencies and at times hearing voices (mostly of the punitive Catholic kind). She'd stopped eating, was blind from a stroke, had survived a series of shock treatments her family had tricked her into consenting to. She endured most forms of degradation and loss a person can imagine. She did not go gently into that good night.

When she died, she was full of a world of anxiety. She believed the world was a terrible and violent place and she worried about how her life would measure in relation to the hierarchy of values and the value of certain lives. She was a deeply religious woman who had survived her three children, one who had suicided at 19, one who had come out as queer at 17, and one who had divorced multiple times—all in her mind sins that could be attributed to her failure as a mother, and which would prevent her from entering heaven.

When I was younger, we were inseparable. She supported me in all my creative endeavors, she in the hard-backed chair in the corner of a friend's living room with her purse in her lap while we sang show tunes around the piano. The price for all of that connection was that I sometimes felt that my mother was devouring me, that I could never differentiate, never leave, never disappoint her. I loved my mother, but I wanted my own life— queer and precarious and free.

She clung to me despite my increasing difference from her, and she mourned with anger the loss of our sameness. It might seem like I'm another ungrateful adoptee, but these things are seldom so

Chen suggests that thinking and feeling with toxicity invites a recounting of the "affectivity and relationality—indeed the bonds—of queerness" (2011, p. 265), which goes beyond current interpretations or enactments of queerness. Returning to queer theoretical roots, but in a posthumanist broadening that includes animal, mineral and a dizzying array of nonhuman subjects, Chen uses 'toxicity' in both literal and figurative ways as a pivot for understanding subjectivity and relationality and the ways in which communion is possible in spite of and because of this affective matrix (p. 277).

So how do queerness and environmental massacres (both micro and macro) mutually inform one another? Chen (2011, 2012) examines toxicity as vulnerability, safety, immunity, intimacy and threat, all of which are sexually and racially instantiated. They write, "Unlike viruses, toxins are not so very containable and quarantinable; they are better thought of as conditions with effects, bringing their own affects and animacies to bear on lives and nonlives" (pp. 281–282).

This suggests that "the queering and racializing of material other than human amounts to a kind of *animacy* . . . built on the recognition that abstract concepts, inanimate objects, and things in between can be queered and racialized without human bodies present" and thus moving beyond simplistic theorizations of the life/death binary (2011, p. 265). Toxicity "meddles" with the boundaries around life and non-life, as well as the boundaries that connect and contain bodies. A *toxic queer bond*, Chen argues, "might complicate utopian imagining, as well as address how and where subject-object dispositions

simple. I was somehow both a desired connection and a toxic contaminant in the hierarchies of virtue and sin.

While I was trying to escape Anna Mae's 'devouring' motherlove, I wanted to find my birthmother with a clawing hunger. I dreamt in images, fleshbodies, my connection to hers like a virus, a mutation.

I wondered what it would feel like to be held by the person from whose body I had come, what it would be like to look into a face like my own. I wondered, trespassed and invited loss as I wrote letter after letter to Dorothy.

Last time I was home in upstate New York, my brother Mark and I went to the old graveyard at St Henry's church and visited the grave of our brother Michael. Afterward, we walked into the old section of the cemetery, talking about how we want others to dispose of our bodies when we're dead. I kept asking Mark what he prefers, but he wouldn't say. I persisted, and finally he said, "I want to be cremated, and taken to the top of the Empire State Building and scattered over the edge, and I want everyone down on the street to breathe me in."

And it was an uncanny moment, because I had only just been reading about the permeability of bodies and buildings and ash. I'd just been reading, "Standing before, I ingest you . . . I am ingesting your exhaled air, your sloughed skin" (Chen 2011, p. 280).

See, we actually do 'consume' one another. Not necessarily in the ways that stories depict mothers devouring their children, but rather in how we might be attributed to the relational queer figure" (p. 265). "In perhaps its best versions, toxicity propels, not repels, queer loves . . . inviting loss and its 'loser,' and trespassing containers of animacy" (p. 281). meddle the boundaries of what's containable, livable. What propels queer love.

Though perhaps we have known that all along.

Love Has Somehow to Rise

What can massacres, both macro and micro, teach us about productive queering of culture, and the inevitable queering of ourselves? Some queer massacres are micro-massacres, "slow death" by mundane annihilations from which we never really recover (Berlant 2007). Others are global, macro, massive—events in which we see in cultural and environmental relief the patterns of individual pain and desire that move ever outward (Schulman 2016). As Chen (2011) notes, "Love has somehow to rise above the social grammar of such encounters" (p. 275). The movement toward affect, emotion, personal narrative, critical autoethnography and empathy for things and animals is surely a response to the move toward 'big data,' the chill of the automation of nearly everything, and its resistant inability to solve the failures of love and relationship that continue to 'queer' the imagined life, as it unfolds in/on/before us.

But there is more here than a dirge. More than massacre and everyday annihilations. More than the "negative toxicity" of "effacement, avoidance, infectious threat, and fear" of our animate encounters with one another (Chen 2011, p. 275). We see queer autoethnography and the move to *queering* autoethnography as a bid to assemble queer spaces—and the "we" that needs and remembers them. It is a claim to count our lives—in all of their precariousness and reliance upon others both human and nonhuman—as animate, livable and grievable. It is a collective call for reparation and for justice by working through, under, beneath and toward a certain kind of hope (Muñoz 2006, p. 687).

Notes

1 It is, of course, impossible to know or assert knowledge about the motivations of any massacre, and the mass shooting by Omar Mateen at the Pulse Nightclub in Orlando, Florida. Regardless of the motivation, it remains the deadliest incident of violence against LGBT people in US history (Orlando nightclub shooting 2018).
2 This section builds on the conceptual argument developed in an earlier version in Harris and Holman Jones (2017).
3 This scene and moment in Delaney's autobiography is the launching point for an argument Joan W. Scott makes in her now-classic essay "The Evidence of Experience" (1991), in which she cautions against using personal experience as evidence of knowledge that is not adequately contextualized and historicized by asking questions about "discourse, difference and subjectivity, as well as about what counts as experience and who gets to make that determination" (1991, p. 790). Scott makes a compelling case

for writing experience in ways that see experience as an event in history and in time and that offer multiple interpretations of the implications of that event for producing subjectivities, discourses and social formations so that we might produce what she calls a "wavering of the visible" (p. 794). Scott's case provides a touchstone for our argument that queering queer autoethnography is a project of making previously invisible experience visible without offering an analysis of the ideological, historical and materials workings of social institutions that perpetuate difference as deficit (p. 779). For more discussion of Delaney's text and Scott's analysis in the context of autoethnographic research, see Holman Jones (2009).

4 Deleuze 1968, p. 100.
5 Pratt 1990, p. 30.
6 Ibid.
7 Berlant 2007, p. 761.
8 Pratt 1990, p. 30.
9 These lines are adapted and reimagined from Pratt 1990, p. 30, who writes, "The flashes of story/brilliant and grim as strobe lights in the dark/the dance shown as grimace/head thrown back in pain."
10 This text is adapted from Butler (2015), who writes: "The discursive invocation of the 'we' refers then to a people whose needs, desires and demands are not yet fully known, and whose coming together is bound up with a future that is yet to be lived out" (p. 169).
11 Chinchilla (2018), p. 8.
12 Ibid.
13 Ibid.
14 Butler (2009), writes: "To frame the frame ... to call the frame into question is to show that the frame never quite contained the scene it was meant to limn, that something was already outside, which made the very sense of the inside possible, recognizable.... Something exceeds the frame that troubles our sense of reality; in other words, something occurs that does not conform to our established understanding of things" (p. 13).
15 While South Dakota's Department of Environment and Natural Resources acknowledged the spill, it did not notify the public (Grenoble 2017).
16 This panic led to a discourse of protecting the middle-class white child from toxic Chinese lead. Highlighting the ironic and racialized opposing truth, Chen (2012) considers that children of color, specifically African American children, and poor and working-class children, are routinely exposed to lead in the paint on the walls in public housing projects in the United States.

References

Ahmed, S. (2006). *Queer phenomenology: Orientations, objects, others*. Durham, NC and London: Duke University Press.

Aho, T., Ben-Moshe, L. & Hilton, L.J. (2017). Mad futures: Affect/theory/violence. *American Quarterly*, 69(2), 291–302.

Berlant, L. (2007). Slow death (sovereignty, obesity, lateral agency). *Critical Inquiry*, 33(4), 754–780.

Butler, J. (2006). *Precarious life: The power of mourning and violence*. New York: Verso.

Butler, J. (2009). *Frames of war: When is life grievable?* Brooklyn, NY: Verso.

Butler, J. (2015). *Notes toward a performative theory of assembly*. Cambridge, MA: Harvard University Press.

Chen, M.Y. (2011). Toxic animacies, inanimate affections. *GLQ: A Journal of Lesbian and Gay Studies*, 17(2–3), 265–286.

Chen, M.Y. (2012). *Animacies: Biopolitics, racial mattering, and queer affect*. Durham, NC and London: Duke University Press.

Chinchilla, M. (2018). Church at night: For Orlando. *GLQ: A Journal of Lesbian and Gay Studies*, 24(1), 3–8.

Dakota Access Pipeline Protests. (2018). *Wikipedia*. https://en.wikipedia.org/wiki/Dakota_Access_Pipeline_protests.

Delaney, S.R. (1988). *The motion of light in water: Sex and science fiction writing in the East Village, 1957–1965*. New York: Arbor House Publishing.

Deleuze, G. (1968). *Difference and repetition*. London and New York: Continuum.

Dickerson, C. (2018, 23 January). What is DACA? Who are the dreamers? Here are some answers. *The New York Times*. www.nytimes.com/2018/01/23/us/daca-dreamers-shutdown.html.

Gambino, L. (2017, 11 March). Native Americans take Dakota access pipeline protest to Washington. *The Guardian*. www.theguardian.com/us-news/2017/mar/10/native-nations-march-washington-dakota-access-pipeline.

Grenoble, R. (2017, 11 May). Dakota access pipeline has already leaked 84 gallons of oil, and it's not even operational yet. *Huffington Post*. www.huffingtonpost.com.au/entry/dakota-access-pipeline-oil-leak_us_5913764be4b021221db9d34b.

Harris, A., & Holman Jones, S. (2017). Feeling fear, feeling queer: The peril and potential of queer terror. *Qualitative Inquiry*, 23(7), 561–568.

Harris, A., Holman Jones, S., Faulkner, S., & Brook, E. (2017). *Queering families, schooling publics: Keywords*. New York: Routledge.

Holman Jones, S. (2009). Crimes against experience. *Cultural Studies <-> Critical Methodologies* 9(5), 608–618.

Holman Jones, S. (2016). Living bodies of thought: The critical in critical autoethnography. *Qualitative Inquiry*, 22(4), 228–237.

Holman Jones, S. (2017). Assembling a we in critical qualitative inquiry. In Denzin, N.K. & Giardina, M.D., eds., *Qualitative inquiry in neoliberal times*, pp. 130–135. New York and London: Routledge.

Hyner, B.H. & Stearns, P.M. (2009). *Forces of nature: natural(-izing) gender and gender(-ing) nature in the discourses of western culture*. Newcastle upon Tyne, UK: Cambridge Scholars Publishing.

Levinas, E. (1996). Peace and proximity. In Peperzak, A.T., Critchley, S. & Bernasconi, R., eds., *Emmanuel Levinas: Basic philosophical writings*, pp. 161–170. Bloomington, IN: Indiana University Press.

Muñoz, J.E. (2006). Feeling brown, feeling down: Latina affect, the performativity of race, and the depressive position. *Signs*, 31(3), 675–688.

Orlando nightclub shooting. (2018). *Wikipedia*. https://en.wikipedia.org/wiki/Orlando_nightclub_shooting.

Pollock, D. (1998). Performing writing. In Phelan, P. & Lane, J., eds., *The ends of performance*, pp. 73–103. New York and London: New York University Press.

Pratt, M.B. (1990). *Crime against nature*. Ithaca, NY: Firebrand Books.

Puar, J. (ed.) (2012). Precarity talk: A virtual roundtable with Lauren Berlant, Judith Butler, Bojana Cvejić, Isabell Lorey, Jasbir Puar, and Ana Vujanović. *The Drama Review*, 56(4), 163–177.

Schulman, Sarah. (2009). *Ties that bind: Familial homophobia and its consequences*. New York: The New Press.

Schulman, Sarah. (2016). *Conflict is not abuse: Overstating harm, community responsibility and the duty of repair*. Vancouver, BC: Arsenal Pulp Press.

Scott, J. (1991). The evidence of experience. *Critical Inquiry*, 17(4), 773–797.

Stewart, K. & Harding, S. (1999). Bad endings: American apocalypse. *Annual Review of Anthropology*, 28, 285–310.

Visser, N. (2017, 6 June). Thousands fought against the Dakota access pipeline. Now it's set to flow oil. *Huffington Post*. www.huffingtonpost.com.au/entry/dakota-access-pipeline-protest-photos_us_592faa01e4b0540ffc847a58.

3

QUEERING MOVEMENTS

Fight for your lives before it's someone else's job.

—(Emma Gonzalez, #MarchForOurLives)

6:20 Between Life and Death

The successive waves of outraged citizens who march against corrupt regimes—in the United States, in Syria, in Palestine, in Australia—begins on this morning to feel like the relentlessness of waves in the ocean. Each one important, to be sure, but inevitably and crushingly followed by another, and another, and another. On this morning, it is #MarchForOurLives, the fierce young survivors of the shooting tragedy at a south Florida school, rousing a country seemingly asleep in Trump-era depression out of its lethargy and into a belief that at least, if we have fallen dangerously asleep, this incoming generation is jaw-droppingly awake. Woke.

On this morning, the millions of young people, teachers, parents and desperate average citizens say 'no more,' and one of them, in a moment that will go down in social movement history, says absolutely nothing, for six minutes and twenty seconds. On this morning, the American president the message is meant for has retired to that same state of Florida, to play golf. He is not afraid of being seen as callous, disrespectful. In fact, he has made his political name on it. The marchers' passion is matched only by his disinterest. On this morning, a world away (and yet not) in Melbourne, Australia, I sit watching Emma Rodriguez offer her crowd two familiar activist and autoethnographic tools: silence, and the power of #SayTheirNames.

It returns me to my own coming of age passions in 1989 New York City, not long after the formation of ACT UP (AIDS Coalition to Unleash Power), and its most famous catch-cry: "Silence Equals Death." Speaking up is important, I learned, as an act of resistance in the face of those individuals and cultures that seek to silence the marginalized. Screaming from the margins can in itself be an act of power, an act of social change, a life-saving act of solidarity for those doing the screaming. But marches can also, we have learned since, be a cathartic 'moment' that fails to materialize into a 'movement' (Harris & Holman Jones 2017 a, b; Harris 2017).

This morning, silence equaled life and respect for the dead. Silence shouted as tears streamed down this Cuban American young woman's face (Simon 2018), and as Emma Gonzalez waited six long minutes and twenty seconds, the length of time it took for the shooter to kill seventeen of her schoolmates and so many lives to be changed forever, as Gonzalez made us all feel the weight of every one of those three hundred eighty seconds, I sat a world away and wept, remembering that not silence, nor its absence, equals death *or* life, but that passion and collectivity will save us, will bring us back when tragedy once again seeks to separate us.

I'm reminded of another response to AIDS and gentrification and other death-making social codes from the 1990s, during my own coming-of-age time: Jonathan Larson's haunting anthem from his blockbuster Broadway musical smash *Rent*, 'Seasons of Love.' That song too reminded us, as a refrain, that measuring a life is elusive yet is deeply rooted in both time and emotion, which Emma Gonzalez brought home to us at the March for Our Lives rally on March 25, 2018.[1] Larson too used time, refrain and silence in his call to honor lives and what makes a 'life worth grieving' (Butler 2009):

> Five hundred and twenty-five thousand, six hundred minutes. . .
> How do you measure,
> Measure a year? . . .
> How do you measure,
> Measure a life?
> In truths that she learned,
> or in times that he cried?
> In bridges he burned,
> or the way that she died?

Larson's lyrics move the listener beyond the constraints of temporality, and toward the ways in which lives matter for their affective and relational reverberations. But what relationship is there between time and life, when—in a material sense—all living things do have a discernible beginning and most certainly do come to an end?

In an age of 'tweetable moments,' where the world circulates the pithy and the visual, Emma Gonzalez brought time to a standstill in her speech in Washington

DC, and she did it with silence, not articulation. She memorialized the lost lives of her friends in minutes, and seconds, and moments that would never be, that would never be repeated, or would now never come. But the world-shattering six minutes and twenty seconds that she commemorates showed us differently from Larson just how short a human life can be, by showing us its corollary: by showing (not telling) how very long those six minutes and twenty seconds were, and how time can be stretched into lifetimes in instances of trauma. Not unlike the victims of the Pulse nightclub in Orlando (also in Florida), Gonzalez's performance brings us into the experience of waiting, not knowing, not speaking, and silently persisting. She shows us that while Silence Equals Death evoked one kind of activist power, silence can also speak louder than all the words in the world.

> In a little over six minutes, seventeen of our friends were taken from us. Fifteen were injured.
> . . . For us, long, tearful chaotic hours in the scorching afternoon sun were spent not knowing.
> No one understood the extent of what had happened.
> No one could believe there were bodies in that building waiting to be identified for over a day.
> No one knew that the people who were missing had stopped breathing long before any of us knew that a code red had been called.
> No one could comprehend the devastating aftermath or how far this would reach or where this would go.
>
> *(qtd. in Tognotti 2018)*

As I watch on my computer the next day, Gonzalez paints a scene for us, a scene that we feel affectively, not visually, not logically, not in any other way than in the solar plexus of fear, loss, not-knowing, and silent waiting alone in that heat. She poignantly moves into #SayTheirNames mode and says the name of every single lost child and what they will never do again, as the crowd begins to cry with her. Name by name. Life by life. Connection by connection. When she reaches the last name, Meadow Pollock, Emma Gonzalez stops speaking, stares steadfastly forward, and while her heavy breathing and tears streaming down her face tell their own story, her silence never wavers.

The audience is uncomfortable. I am uncomfortable, here in Australia. The large crowd waits uneasily with this silence, although Gonzalez's steely gaze and confidence show undeniably that she is not lost, not overcome, and that this silence is completely intentional. Periodically people chant, rouse, clap and cheer her on with shouts like, "We love you Emma!" and "Right here with you Emma!" She doesn't move. Her chest rises and falls with the waxing and waning breath of heartbreak. It is impossible to look away from her, as we try to wait with as much steadfastness as she does. Her silence and stance feel ritualistic: Is she re-enacting the agony of that six minutes and twenty seconds of fear and not knowing? Is she enacting an overdue 'fuck you' to the shooter? Is she saying goodbye to each of those friends, silently here with us, because she was unable to do so on the day it happened? Whatever is going through the mind of Emma Gonzalez as we all wait together, the waiting is a meditation, both a stillness and a collective silent rage on a global scale against the atomization of gun violence; it is an intentional elongation of time in the face of tragedy that can so brutally cut everything short.

After this unbearably long collective silence, her phone alarm goes off. We all jump, it comes so out of the blue, but Gonzalez is calm and measured as she turns it off and turns back to us: "Since the time that I came out here, it's been six minutes and twenty seconds," she says. "The shooter has ceased shooting and will soon abandon his rifle, blend in with the students as they escape, and walk free for an hour before arrest. Fight for your lives before it's someone else's job" (qtd in Tognotti). Finally, and although I'd read about this speech a dozen times before watching it, and knew exactly what to expect intellectually, a kind of cumulative devastation rises up in my chest and the sobs escape from my throat. While sometimes I feel I've become increasingly cynical about the possibility of structural political change in this world, today Gonzalez reminds me that stories matter, time matters, matter matters, and collective ritual changes us before we can change anything else. Through the circuitry of networked digital media, Gonzalez changed global attention to gun violence through telling her story of survival.

Time and More-Than-Time[2]

Erin Manning claims, "time is not endured. It is activated" (2009, p. 24). In writing about Australian Indigenous artmaking and the Dreamtime origin stories, which are the narratives and material worldings that underpin all Indigenous knowledge, she observes that

> the Dreaming cooperates on both the virtual and the actual strata [and is] emphasized by the Dreaming's adherence to a non-linear cycle of time, where what returns is not "time-as-it-was" but "time-as-it-will-become." This is a time of the future-past, a present in the making. The relationship between the forces of movement's intensive magnitude and the extensive continuum creates space-times of experience through which the return returns.
>
> *(2009, p. 201)*

For Manning, time is a provocation for worldings to occur. Emergence is always the present moment. As such, the present in the making always already contains within it a 'future-past' that is evocative but not statically tied to any objective notion of a kind of time which passes; rather, time is an experience, an affect, a constituent part of an emergence rather than a marker or a recorder of some-thing *that happened*. As autoethnographers, we tell and are surrounded by "truths too hard and complex to represent with a meme, and their counter-stories that claim they are all lies" (Harris 2017, p. 24). Autoethnography can be an inventing, "not recording or evoking" (p. 25). Moments of social upheaval and coming together like the #MarchForOurLives and Emma Gonzalez's speech are collective emergences that are most alive in their present-in-the-making, both virtual and actual, but sometimes struggle to convert from 'marches' to social movements, which require a kind of return. In ruptures or intensities like the Emma Gonzalez moment, time becomes both timeless and *timeful*. It is both 'time-as-it-was' and also time of the future-past. Its electricity, its *frisson*, is exactly a result of the collective sense of stepping out of time. In so doing, Gonzalez is not only slapping down the American president, the gun lobby, the older generation and the shooter, but also death itself, and—by extension—time as the engine of death.

Yet time and even death, as metaphysical poets like John Donne have reminded us, can be conquered in multiple ways.[3] In his poem "Death, be not proud," the speaker tells Death he is not as powerful as he thinks he is. The speaker anthropomorphizes Death, blurring the lines between human and nonhuman. Death itself will die, because (for Christians) eternal life takes all the punch out of death, reduces it to more of a temporary state than an eternal one. He calls Death a slave to other forces: fate, chance, kings and desperate men, taunting while he warns Death against pride, saying Death's supposed power is an illusion, fleeting. He says Death's pride in its power is a dangerous folly. Such rhetorical devices are used every day in contemporary social movements, and sometimes in autoethnography. Gonzalez and the other speakers that day took exactly such a tone, warning the establishment that this kind of gun violence will not continue, that the arrogance of lobby groups like the National Rifle Association will no longer hold sway in lawmaking across the nation, and that the apathy of this generation of lawmakers is a folly, is false and is coming to an end.

Like activists, Donne and the other metaphysical poets of the 17th century focused more on the spoken than the written power of language. Like social movements and social media that globalizes them, the metaphysical style was highly adaptable to fit contemporary forms, issues and cultural conditions and combined poetic with common language, specifically unlikely or paradoxical mash-ups. The style deployed humor, puns, rhetorical cleverness and complexity, hyperbole (or 'conceits') and repetition, again sharing much with social movement strategies (especially as enacted online) of today.

But of course the metaphysical poets were also concerned with spiritual or philosophical questions, questions of existence, the meaning of life, and passionately and rigorously exploring questions of right behavior, relationality and connection (to self, to 'god,' to others), in the same ways that autoethnography and social movements seek to connect the personal and cultural, seek deeper meaning from everyday life, see the macro in the micro of personal narrative and animating our connections to all that is around us. The metaphysical poets like Donne might have been evocative autoethnographers; they were certainly critical autoethnographers, too (Harris & Holman Jones 2016), seeking connection and meaning very much through a critique of the status quo. They understood the double-edged sword of catharsis, of feelings, of affect. Autoethnography and personal witness in social movements *queer time* by calling out to something timeless, universal, limitless.

Spacetime and Social Movements

But time and space intersect in social movements in particular ways. And in so doing, place itself becomes a ritual, place evokes the previous events that have occurred there, the collectivities, and as such "creates space-times of experience through which the return returns" (Manning 2009, p. 201).

In his "Letter from Birmingham Jail," in response to those in his own civil rights movement who urged him to wait, to give it time, Martin Luther King Jr. wrote that his comrades suffered from a

> tragic misconception of time, from the strangely irrational notion that there is something in the very flow of time that will inevitably cure all ills. Actually, time itself is neutral; it can be used either destructively or constructively. More and more I feel that the people of ill will have used time much more effectively than have the people of good will. . . . Time itself becomes an ally of the forces of social stagnation. We must use time creatively, in the knowledge that the time is always ripe to do right.
>
> *(King 1963)*

King reminds us that there is no such thing as 'well-timed' social movements or revolutions; that the status quo seeks inaction and patience, and that social rebellion and social change always require impatience and action, as Emma Gonzalez reminded us more recently. King says,

> Frankly, I have yet to engage in a direct-action campaign that was 'well timed' in the view of those who have not suffered . . . for years now I have heard the word 'Wait!' It rings in the ear of every Negro with piercing familiarity. This 'wait' has almost always meant 'never.' We must come to see . . . that 'justice too long delayed is justice denied.'
>
> *(King 1963, p. 173)*

For King, Birmingham was one site which has since become spacetime resonant with the ritual power of what happened there in the civil rights movement, but which caused it to become a mythical place beyond its material existence.

Selma, Alabama, is another. On March 5, 2017, 54 years after King's "Letter from Birmingham Jail," then-President Barack Obama spoke at the 50th anniversary of King's march on Selma. On that day, Obama reflected, "There are places and moments in America where this nation's destiny has been decided" (qtd. in Rhodan 2015). He reminded us that Selma (and other places of ritualized unity and resistance) is not a "museum or static monument to behold from a distance" but rather "a living thing, a call to action, a roadmap for citizenship" (Rhodan 2015).

And then he spoke directly to a new generation of activists, like soon-to-be activist Emma Gonzalez, when he said, "this generation of young people can draw strength from this place, where the powerless could change the world's greatest superpower, and push their leaders to expand the boundaries of freedom," acknowledging the symbolic power of places themselves as calls-to-action (qtd. in Rhodan 2015). The National Mall in Washington DC, stretching from the capitol on one end to the Lincoln Memorial on the other, is another such place.

It is where in 2018 Emma Gonzalez stood, eyes fixed, for six minutes and twenty seconds and the world stood with her. The same place where, on August 28, 1963, Martin Luther King Jr. gave his famous "I Have a Dream" speech during the March on Washington for Jobs and Freedom, on the steps of the Lincoln Memorial. Both Gonzalez and King used time as a rhetorical device for urging people to act, King with the refrain, "now is the time." In 2009, at his first inauguration, Obama used this same device in calling a divided America together with the phrase, "the time has come." And in closing he spoke to a "future world," to "our children's children." He evoked just that "non-linear cycle of time, where what returns is not 'time-as-it-was' but 'time-as-it-will-become'" (2009, p. 201) which Erin Manning conjures, a spacetime that is a temporal and material emergence only in the now.

Silence and Social Change

I remember arriving in Washington DC late on the evening of Monday, January 19, 2009, the night before Barack Obama's first euphoric inauguration, as he became the first African American president.

> I remember the crisp air, the biting cold.
> I remember fearing that he would be assassinated before he could even take office.
> I remember walking from the hotel along silent streets as the snow fell.
> I remember the idling buses and buses and buses bearing license plates from every corner of this country.
> I remember the young people helping old people out of those buses and cars, trains, and vans, every race mingling under that black night sky.
> I remember walking along the wrought iron fence in front of the White House and passing small groups of people of every age, race, gender, huddled,
> holding small flickering candles and

the muffled voices, laughter, singing, "We Shall Overcome."
I remember the tears rolling down my face, as yet more buses
rolled silently slowly past, along snow-blanketed streets.
I remember eyes meeting the eyes of strangers, wide open,
as we passed,
wondering if it was ever like this before, or if it would ever be like this
again.
I remember strangers talking to strangers, inviting us in.
I remember people making signs on any surface available,
marks of hope and celebration.
I remember wondering why it was so quiet, was it a reverent silence,
almost spiritual, ritual, religious silence of respect and awe?
Or was it a silence of fear and apprehension, a people afraid of waking the
giant of racist violence against this one moment of fulfilled dreams?
I remember the old people telling us what it was like here in 1963 at
King's "I Have a Dream" speech, and that famous march for civil rights.
Elders, preaching, sharing, autoethnographizing,
just on that quiet famous street, people gathering to hear the wisdom.
Teaching like teaching should be.
Despite the cold.
I remember feeling a part of something bigger than identity politics.
I remember people fundraising to get the forebears here.
I remember people stepping off buses after a week on the road, stretching
legs, looking around as if they were seeing democracy for the first time.
I remember standing at the Lincoln Memorial that night and singing with
strangers like they were family.
I remember wondering if this was what it felt like when Lincoln freed the
slaves.
I remember hoping he didn't get shot.
I remember feeling sad that Reagan and Bush were so eager to let all my
tribe die of AIDS if this is (also) who we are as a nation.
I remember the next day the bitter bitter cold and people carrying old
people because their joints wouldn't work.
I remember Yo-Yo Ma being criticized for recording his performance,
because it was so cold he was afraid his cello would not hold tune.
I remember security so high that after all this, after all this time, after
slavery, after lifetimes, after civil rights, after all this silence, after all the loss,
after all the months of preparation and travel, after everything, I remember
African American elders being stuck in the tunnels underneath the Mall,
trying against the crowds and the few entry points, trying and failing to
reach the sunlight before Obama's speech. I remember their telling of
everyone stopping, joining hands in that dark tunnel, and listening to the
broadcast above them as best they could.

Disappointment not consuming their respect and awe.

Being present.

Meeting the conditions of the moment.

Timeless/timeful.

I remember that when we tried to leave after the speech and everything was over, that my knees wouldn't bend and that I had to step carefully to not fall over and wondering if this is what it feels like to be old, and

I remember the push to get out of that Mall with so few openings in the police fences, that people began to panic, and some people began to preach,

"This is not what Obama has called us to do. Patience people!"

I remember everyone stopped. The quiet returned. Eyes met eyes.

I remember helping lift old people down over the walls to get them out of the crush.

I remember the change in the air on that inauguration day which became about the limitations of achievement, and

I remember missing the stillness and awe of the night before.

That night of readiness potential[4]

That night of preacceleration.[5]

That night of apprehension

Of "is this what it feels like when dreams come true?"

Of we are actually all the same

Of you are my brother

Of give a sister a hand.

Of love

Of love without borders.

"Five hundred and twenty-five thousand, six hundred minutes. . .

How do you measure,

Measure a life?"

The Queer Not-Yet: A Logic of Futurity

Jack Halberstam argues that "queer subcultures produce alternative temporalities . . . by allowing their participants to believe that their futures can be imagined according to logics that lie outside of the conventional," and in some ways contemporary social movements have taken up this call to a future outside of the conventional (2003, p. 4). But how does autoethnography queer social movements, even while social movements are queering majoritarian culture? Halberstam tells us, "queer uses of time and space develop in opposition to the institutions of family, heterosexuality and reproduction" (2003, p. 4), but today's social movements—unlike those like ACT UP—are not always so pointed. They are linked in their commitment to opposing the business as usual of capitalist life, yet often they don't see the intersectionality of oppressions advocated by those like Martin

Luther King Jr., Obama or others as the only way to make lasting structural change. For queer theorists and queer autoethnographers, these intersections point a way forward that, as Barad advocates, recommits to moving beyond binaries completely, and is not reproductive of existing social inequities (Barad 2015). There is no "I" versus an imagined "you"; no us versus them; no objective versus subjective reality, only (recalling Manning) a collective emergence.

Long before trans★ visibility and the (almost global) dawn of 'marriage equality,' Halberstam reminded us that "queer kinship itself has a complex relation to reproduction, cultural production and assimilation" (2003, p. 4). Halberstam articulates queer culture as inextricably linked to popular culture and social resistance including riot dyke bands, drag kings and queer slam poets (2005). Despite today's assimilation of so much of LGBTIQ (if not queer) culture, these subcultural elements and subjectivities continue to proliferate (online and offline), showing the ways in which their autoethnographic nature remains gloriously diverse and divergent. By queering the time and place in which chosen identities and relationships are now possible, hybrid online/offline lives and social movements point toward emergent notions and uses of critical and queer autoethnographies (Harris & Holman Jones 2016).

For Halberstam, "queer subcultures" are queer assemblages that "carve out new territory for a consideration or overlap of gender, generation, class, race, community and sexuality in relation to minority cultural production" (2003, p. 6). Queer theory and queer autoethnography cannot be separated; indeed, queer lives are the material foundations and the 'so what' of queer theory, for without real change, as in social movements, the emergence of the transformative moment is only an idea, not a present in the making.

Places are, as discussed in Chapter 1, becoming monuments, and as such become parts of movements. Places evoke not only past events and victories, but also past leaders, past solidarities, past survivals. At times of celebration and times of trauma, people flock to them, to evoke the foundations of the past upon which we stand in new social movements, but also to very materially and ritualistically bring that past into the *now* of a current emergent social movement.

For queer people, the world, Greenwich Village and specifically the Stonewall Inn is one of those spacetimes. Many people gathered there in 2011 when marriage equality became a reality in New York State, and again on June 26, 2015, when the US Supreme Court ruled that marriage without discrimination based on gender was a national right protected under the United States constitution.

In Australia, marriage equality took longer and followed a different route. Marriage equality was achieved by a controversial postal vote involving all voters, which cost an outrageous 22 million Australian dollars, and raised harmful homophobic and transphobic rhetoric in the media. Most queer community members were outspokenly against the postal vote, but Prime Minister Malcolm Turnbull was unwilling to make the executive order to have the legislative change considered in Parliament without it, fearing he would be 'blamed' for bringing in marriage equality. From September to November 2017, the postal vote was open and the results announced on November 14.

In the lead-up, LGBTIQ organizations put considerable systems in place for the day the results were to be announced, in the event that the vote went against us. If nothing else, queer people know about weathering storms. The level of apprehension and fear was almost unbearable. For those like us, having lived through it already in the United States, now having to be subject to legislative and popular opinion once again was excruciating.

They announced the results of the postal vote when we were in Amsterdam traveling for work. Amsterdam, the city of progressive politics, of legal marijuana, of sexual liberation. It's also a beautiful city full of time, silence and esthetic and political ambivalence. A place of both history and the always-now.

It feels so weird to be away from home at another historical moment for queer politics. It seems to be my fate, I say.

We try to not care about the results announcement, believing it either would go against us or, even if it did go our way, would not be enacted into law.

> Yet they did announce it, and the vote had passed in favor of 'gay marriage.'
> Let's celebrate, we say.
> It doesn't take long to see a rainbow flag hanging in a front window
> Of a comfortingly-seedy bar.
> Must be gay, we agree and leave our meander along another restive canal.
> When we open the front door there is only one other customer at the bar,
> And the bartender; both are male-presenting.
> We say hello and order wine.
> We're celebrating, we tell them.
> No response.
> We're celebrating that today in Australia, where we live, a horribly
> biased process of postal vote at least somehow resulted in a YES vote for
> marriage equality, and we're really happy and relieved.
> Oh, congratulations, they say.
> Thanks, we say, and we all toast.
> We sit quietly looking around while Queen plays on the juke box.
> The place is covered in photos of divas, which seems like a good sign,
> given it is one of our shared passions.
> We share the moment of joy with virtual friends in lieu of any show of
> solidarity from these two corporeal bodies.
> We toast to Barbra, Diana Ross, Cher, Judy, Madonna, Kylie Minogue,
> Lady Gaga, Aretha Franklin, Christina Aguilera, J-Lo, others.
> We think about queer histories, and herstories, and the ways in which
> they get forgotten and made and remembered and superseded.

We think about so many of our tribe who hate everything assimilationist the marriage equality movement stands for, and yet how many of our tribe have lost everything after a shared lifetime, because of a lack of legal protections when one partner dies.

About how laws matter.

And laws change.

About how many of our tribe have fought for so long and never thought it would arrive in our lifetimes.

We think about Obama, in Selma, saying:

> If you think nothing's changed in the past fifty years, ask somebody who lived through the Selma or Chicago or L.A. of the Fifties. Ask the female CEO who once might have been assigned to the secretarial pool if nothing's changed. Ask your gay friend if it's easier to be out and proud in America now than it was thirty years ago. To deny this progress—our progress—would be to rob us of our own agency; our responsibility to do what we can to make America better.
>
> *(qtd. in Rhodan 2015)*

We want to believe in this call to progress;

We have seen it with our own eyes, and yet.

We are weary. And we remember what it has cost. And we remember how easily civil rights can be eroded too.

But on this night

We celebrate because without it we are lost.

We think about queer time and place and most of all queer love.

The timelessness of queer love.

The beauty of the queer not-yet.

Queer futurities and utopias (Halberstam 2005; Muñoz 2009) can seem almost naive at a time when gender fluidity and queer assimilation are experienced alongside a rising tide of anti-LGBTIQ legislation. Muñoz writes that "queerness's form is utopian" (2009, p. 30), that "queerness is an ideality" (p. 1) and that "what we will really know as queerness, does not yet exist" (p. 22). His words are a balm in an increasingly commodified queer life. But they challenge.

Muñoz draws on Martin Heidegger to describe a queer imaginary in which a not-yet is nevertheless a powerful destroyer of the already-is where

> 'time and space are not co-ordinate. Time is prior to space.' If time is prior to space, then we can view both the force of the no-longer-conscious and the not-yet-here as potentially bearing on the *here* of naturalized space and time.
>
> *(2009, p. 29, emphasis in original)*

Muñoz demands the full potential of queer as an intervention, rather than a destination or an identification. Similarly, social movements and galvanizing activists like Emma Gonzalez rely on this not-yet, in order to motivate others who might be *not-yet-affected* by trauma or death-making policies, to demand they fight for something they cannot yet see. For Muñoz, "this 'we' does not speak to a merely identitarian logic but instead to a logic of futurity" (p. 20). Queerness as futurity itself.

Muñoz urges us toward a future that is both utopian but also a "spatial and temporal destination" (p. 85). Unlike Manning's spacetime, Muñoz futurity is not only an enactment but also an ontological dare. It is both *of* temporality and spatiality, and out of time and space. Queer activists and autoethnographers rely on futures that are past/future and time/space, and on the investment of others to share in our vision and enactments of those journeys of/toward those futures, for if they are not collective the social project does not work, be it autoethnographic, activist, or queer.

★

Three weeks later, on December 7, 2017, Australia became the 25th country to adopt same-sex marriage, after going out of its way in 2004 to change the law to make legal marriage between only a man and a woman. On this day, we are both at work and decide to meet in the city to celebrate. The final *final* end to an interminably long process of debate and dehumanization. Despite the positive result in the costly postal vote, it was a non-binding victory and the government was still not obligated to pass it as law. Debates in Parliament had been raging for weeks, and today was the day but the time was unclear. There was talk of a (another) rally at the State Library in downtown Melbourne, as in other cities around the country. This was the culmination of so many years of pain, struggle and collective hopes, but the government kept us guessing and on the back foot until the very last minute.

> Having missed so many other important moments in our recent queer history, we were not going to miss this one.
> We meet at the library and walk to a nearby bar.
> As we sit and order, one of us says, "Let's check to see where things are at" and click on the "stream Parliamentary debate" link.
> Sitting at a table at the back of this dark bar called The Moat, which is decidedly not gay; no gay icons or divas in sight.
> Just as soon as the stream begins, someone says something online in Parliament, an indistinguishable and banal statement of some kind, and suddenly everyone in Parliament is standing, crying, starting to hug.
> "Is that it? Is that it? Is it happening?!" we shout to each other, and somehow to the random others who are seated around us.
> "That's it!" Stacy shouts.

"Oh my god!" Anne cries.

We start to hug, trying not to lose the connection on our phone in case, once again, we were too eager and had misread the signals.

People around us hug each other and congratulate us. It is a moment of solidarity with non-queer others.

"That's it! It's happened! Finally."

The tears flow. We are so glad, at least, to be together, and to be here at home for this one.

This milestone/not-milestone.

This future-past emergence.

This moment where love (or capitalism) wins.

We hug strangers in the bar. We hug each other again.

It is hard to know how to feel and what to do.

We recall moments of grief and joy, like Washington, like New York, for in these moments grief and joy feel similar in their overwhelming emotion.

We finish our drinks and rush to the

lawn of the State Library, the site of so many of the marriage equality and other social movement marches in recent times.

Surely there will be a parade, we think, and surely it will start from here.

But when we get to the lawn, we can't see anyone else who looks Gay-happy.

A quiet early summer evening, rain threatening.

The debates had been expected to go on longer into the night, and so perhaps the parade has been postponed,

maybe until a drier time, maybe until a more predictable time.

But no, surely, we imagine.

Surely *this* day, and *this* time, the spiritual force of solidarity, of victory after the long wait, will bring people out into the streets.

As we do; as we have always done.

We look, and wait. We stand around.

It is an average Thursday evening. A banal evening.

Finally, we see two older women sitting at a bus shelter with a rainbow flag.

Congratulations! We all spontaneously shout.

I hug one of the women.

Do you know each other? Our companions ask.

No! we laugh, joined in the moment, like that cold night in Washington DC before Obama's inauguration.

Another time when we felt the *need*, not the choice, the spontaneous need to be out in the streets and together.

Where is everyone? We ask each other.

We can't believe no one has come.

Two twenty-somethings join us.

We commiserate, check phones, confirm there had been no clear updates.

Someone reads that the celebratory march has been rescheduled, at the last minute, for the next day.

We look at each other and wait. We stand around.

It feels hard to leave this place, this becoming monument.

We are bonded in our *activist affect*, a kind of post-traumatic stress disorder that keeps us on-call, keeps us geared up, but also keeps us keenly aware of the need for and privilege of celebrating the victories, *together*. Because celebrate we must, and we cannot afford the luxury of cynicism, as Obama has said, when there is still so much work to be done.

Autoethnography and Activist Affects

Jeanette Winterson reminds us how "every political movement begins as a counter-narrative to an existing narrative" (2016). This is true for so much autoethnography. Queer autoethnography is itself a resistant tune, sung as new words to old songs that have elided the stories of queer storytellers. But this chapter is also about the need for a *queering* of autoethnography, an evolution in which the story as enactment becomes something more than a recording of past events.

The need for (and power of) autoethnography and social movements is in their shared strategies of telling others and ourselves the stories we desperately need to hear, but not as only witnessing. Autoethnography is just one in a range of queer tools that "speaks truth to power," and in the speaking enacts new worldings, not just records them. Both autoethnography and/in social movements, like queer subcultures, offer important "counter-publics" from which we "model other modes of being and becoming that scramble our understandings of place, time, development, action and transformation" (Halberstam 2003, p. 331).

From the wave of splinter 'movements' that grew out of 2011's Occupy Wall Street movement (Occupy Museums, Occupy Sandy, etc.), the collectivist cry of "We are the 99%," has come to blend personal-as-political narratives, and to queer dominant culture, in new ways. From Pussy Riot to Women's March pussy hats, what does it mean to queer a social movement, and how do the personal and collective work together in social movements (online *and* offline) differently than in other queerly autoethnographic communities?

We recognize the notion of an *activist affect*[6] is in part what queers live with every day. The rolling social movements that appear to be sweeping the globe are simply a democratization of generations of queer resistance gone viral. Today, citizens know that their lives are in danger when they are not able to—or not seen to—contribute to global capitalism. This has bred in the general public a kind of outrage that they too live precarious lives, while in previous generations, white capitalist heteronormative subjects may have had the luxury of believing that they were "safe." Today, no one is safe. It has created a kind of activist zeitgeist of speaking out (albeit sometimes through the 'armchair activism' of social media) and resistance, or what the #MarchForOurLives movement calls the time of "No more!"

But what is an activist affect? It can range from intensities on the skin to the air of a gathering march; the stillness in a room when a genderqueer person enters and is unintelligible to others; the queering of "family time" when we reunite with family members whose silences (and even absences) remind us of the invisibility of some forms of queerness in heteronormative eyes (Halberstam 2005, p. 79). But what is a queering of affect for contemporary activism? Muñoz has described in affective terms how "we may never touch queerness, but we can feel it as the warm illumination of a horizon imbued with potentiality," that queerness is a lens "that can be distilled from the past and used to imagine a future" (2009, p. 1). Queerness, like activism, is a way of being, a mode, a perspective, an enactment of citizenship and a not-yet.

Many activists, like many queers, live an affect of "outrage fatigue," the tipping point reached when one begins to realize that rage itself is not enough. So many outrages occur to those who live in ways that might be considered 'awake' to social injustice, in the present times, that we oscillate between the numbness of overexposure and the rage of still feeling each violation. Where is a bearable place to rest? What is an appropriate ongoing response to unacceptable abuses? Judith Butler (2004) has taken these questions out of the realm of the abstract and reminded us how central they are to peaceful co-existence:

> What makes for a livable world is no idle question. It is not merely a question for philosophers. It is posed in various idioms all the time by people in various walks of life. If that makes them all philosophers, then that is a conclusion I am happy to embrace. It becomes a question for ethics, I think, not only when we ask the personal question, what makes my own life bearable, but when we ask, from a position of power, and from the point of view of distributive justice, what makes, or ought to make, the lives of others bearable?
>
> *(Butler 2004, p. 17)*

Queer people continue to suffer bias, discrimination, alienation and at times work, housing and financial oppression. In earlier days of queer liberation, the 1969 Stonewall rebellion through the ACT UP years of AIDS activism, queer rage and queer activism had a galvanizing effect within queer (and other) communities, offering energy and solidarity in resistance to the unequal treatment of all minoritarian people through death-making governmental policies. The catharsis of queer activism helped many of us survive, and process the everyday micro- and macro-aggressions with which we lived.

Those years provided both deep sorrow and fear as a coming-of-age queer woman in New York City, discovering gayness at a time when that community was characterized by death, fear and protests. But there was also incredible joy and solidarity between queer men, women and others, a kind of unity that sometimes feels lost today in the queer community, but perhaps more widely seen in the rolling social movements like #BlackLivesMatter and the #MarchForOurLives. As aging queer and gender diverse people, we ask ourselves, what is the place of catharsis in real social change? The function of rage? Do these feelings keep us alive, spur us to action, or dissipate the energy, force and emotion that might be used elsewhere?

Autoethnographic and activist practices continue their interdependent trajectories in ways that suggest a queering of activist movements might have more to do with de-commodifying than sexuality or gender margins. From New York City's *Centre for Artistic Activism* (Lambert 2014), to the *Creative Activists Toolkit* (CAT), to Naomi Klein's large-scale *This Changes Everything*, to the craft-led "slow activism/slow art" of community-based movements, the threads of autoethnography and activism are intertwined in both affective and collectivist ways. Like autoethnography, activism today is a way of building community, a practice, a philosophy, reiterating the links between personal narrative, participatory culture, community organizing and civic engagement.

In a saturated media environment weary of big events and relentless political and social upheaval, storytelling through autoethnographic activism emotionally re-engages bystanders with protest movements that—sometimes inspiring, sometimes irritating—continue long-term efforts in a short attention span world. Like the power of Emma Gonzalez's survival narrative, personal narrative offers a feeling of real connection across miles—like we felt when we watched it here in Australia online. Gonzalez used all the most effective tools of autoethnographic methods: personal and cultural commentary, intertwined; silence juxtaposed with repetition and other effective rhetorical devices; a call to action to a culture that has fallen asleep, a cry for us to look more critically at ourselves, to take more action, to find freedom from this current oppression through unity, through community, through emotionally bonded collectivity.

Queer/ing Social Futures

The 'queering culture' potential of social movements brings us back to the personal. Julie Norman (2009), Sanjay Asthana (2015) and others have detailed the role of social media for creating global communities amidst the single story: Palestinian youth activists, rural trans* youth, Syrian refugees. Autoethnography queers activist and social movement scholarship by linking the personal and political in more transparently affective ways. Such emotional and creative strategies are more visible than ever since, for example, 2010's Arab Spring uprising, the "indignados" protests in Spain, the global Occupy movement, Hong Kong's

"Umbrella Revolution," #BlackLivesMatter, the Women's March movement, and the #MarchForOurLives with which we started this chapter. Autoethnography queers the research landscape too, in ways that parallel the intersectional social movements we examine in this chapter, and is well-situated to highlight the inter-relatedness of the personal and political in networked cultures (Bloch 2015).

So we ask: How can autoethnography help queer social movements, subcultures and cultural stories, as social movements continue to queer autoethnography? Extending Halberstam (2005) and Muñoz (2009), we understand queer utopian futurities to be ones in which all those who reject the mainstream can gather, self-represent, and change culture—both in our homonormative near future and in the utopian future that is the not-yet. Unlike activists from previous eras, activists today spend much of their time participating in highly personal, hybrid and creative communities through online engagement, marching and "DIY making" activities around shared values and politics. This is not unlike autoethnographers who mix a range of creative strategies to queer mainstream scholarship through a recognition of the co-constitutive emergence of self and culture. Both social movement scholarship and autoethnography, as inherently political interventions in the academy, are global communities of practice networked in democratized and de-centralized ways, shared with and galvanizing their communities within seconds, and which offer the possibility of massive "real-world impact" like never before.

Autoethnography offers one way of queering academic work as the spread of digital media and online representation has made us hungrier than ever for personal connection. While it remains true that not all have equal access to the internet (Fuchs 2014; Castells 2014), issues of access are central to both autoethnographers and hybrid social movement organizers like Emma Gonzalez, who remind us of the future-past potential of massacres and movements; how one more mass shooting in the United States could enact Muñoz's and Halberstam's queer futurities, the kind of autoethnographic rupture that "No one could comprehend" as a cultural pivot, the reverberating silence of survival, or "the devastating aftermath or how far this would reach or where this would go" (Gonzalez qtd. in Tognotti). For them and for us, the emergent not-yet is both queer and decidedly activist.

Notes

1 In June 2018, drama students at Marjory Stoneman Douglas High School in Parkland Florida, sang 'Seasons of Love' on the Tony Awards stage in tribute honouring Melody Herzfeld, the drama teacher who saved 65 lives by barricading students in a classroom closet. Herzfeld later encouraged these same students to lead the call for gun reform, including the nationwide March For Our Lives demonstration (Associated Press 2018). In addition to the moving tribute offered by the survivors, Herzfeld was honoured with a special award for educators (Michaud & Serjeant 2018).

2 For more from Anne about the relationship between time, place and action, see Harris 2015.

3 "Death be not proud, Holy Sonnet X" of the 19 holy sonnets (Donne 1633).

4   Schmidt 2015.
5   Manning 2009.
6   We more fulsomely theorize the concept of an *activist affect* in *The Queer Life of Things* (Holman Jones & Harris, forthcoming), which blends new materialist, affect and autoethnographic theoretics to look critically at activism in contemporary culture.

References

Associated Press. (2018, 10 June). Florida school shooting survivors sing at Tony Awards. *New York Post*. https://nypost.com/2018/06/10/florida-school-shooting-survivors-sing-at-emmy-awards/

Asthana, S. (2015). Youth, self, other: A study of Ibdaa's digital media practices in the West Bank, Palestine. *Journal of Cultural Studies*, 20(1), 100–117.

Barad, K. (2015). Transmaterialities: Trans★/matter/realities and queer political imaginings. *GLQ: A Journal of Lesbian and Gay Studies*, 21(2–3), 387–422.

Bloch, N. (2015, 8 January). The arts of protest: The art of #Black lives matter. *Waging Nonviolence, People-powered News & Analysis*. http://wagingnonviolence.org/feature/art-blacklivesmatter/

Butler, J. (2004). *Undoing gender*. New York/London: Routledge.

Butler, J. (2009). *Frames of war: When is life grievable?* New York: Verso Books.

Castells, M. (2014). Networks of outrage and hope: social movements in the internet age. *Media, Culture & Society*, 36(1), 122–124.

Creative activists' tool kit. www.slideshare.net/CharlesGYF/the-creative-activist-toolkit.

Donne, J. (1633). Death, be not proud. www.poets.org/poetsorg/poem/death-be-not-proud-holy-sonnet-10.

Fuchs, C. (2014). Book review: Manuel Castells, Networks of Outrage and Hope: Social movements in the internet age. *Media, Culture & Society*, 36(1), 122–124.

Halberstam, J. (2003). What's that smell? Queer temporalities and subcultural lives. *International Journal of Cultural Studies*, 6(3), 313–333.

Halberstam, J. (2005). *In a queer time and place: Transgender bodies, subcultural lives*. New York/London: New York University Press.

Harris, A. (2015). Twice upon a place. *Applied Theatre Research Journal*, 3(1), 5–19.

Harris, A. (2017). An adoptee autoethnographic femifesta. *International Review of Qualitative Research*, 10(1), 24–28.

Harris, A. & Holman Jones, S. (2016). Living bodies of thought: The critical in critical autoethnography. *Qualitative Inquiry*, 22(2), 228–237.

Harris, A. & Holman Jones, S. (2017a). Feeling fear, feeling queer: The peril and potential of queer terror. *Qualitative Inquiry*, 23(7), 561–568.

Harris, A. & Holman Jones, S. (2017b). I am a monument. In Holman Jones, S. & Pruyn, M., eds., *Creative selves/creative cultures: Critical autoethnography, performance, and pedagogy*, pp. 113–130. New York: Palgrave Macmillan.

Harris, A., & Holman Jones, S. (2019, forthcoming). *The queer life of things: Performance, affect, and the more-than-human*. Lanham, MD: Lexington Books.

Holman Jones, S. & Harris, A. (forthcoming). Activist affect. *Qualitative Inquiry*.

King, M.L., Jr. (1963). Letter from Birmingham jail. www.africa.upenn.edu/Articles_Gen/Letter_Birmingham.html

Lambert, S. (2014). Interview with the Center for Creative Activism. http://we-make-money-not-art.com/archives/2014/03/interview-with-center-for-creative-activism.php#.U79RtP2Ks_s

Manning, E. (2009). *Relationscapes: Movement, art, philosophy*. Boston: MIT Press.

Michaud, C. & Serjeant, J. (2018, 11 June). Florida shooting survivors get standing ovation at Tony awards. *Reuters*. https://www.reuters.com/article/us-awards-tonys-shooting/florida-shooting-survivors-get-standing-ovation-at-tony-awards-idUSKBN1J705S

Muñoz, J. E. (2009). *Cruising utopia: The then and there of queer futurity*. New York/London: New York University Press.

Norman, J.M. (2009). Creative activism: Youth media in Palestine. *Middle East Journal of Culture and Communication*, 2(2), 251–274.

Rhodan, M. (2015, 7 March). Transcript: Read full text of President Barack Obama's speech in Selma. *Time Magazine Online*. http://time.com/3736357/barack-obama-selma-speech-transcript/

Schmidt, T. (2015). Some people will do anything to keep themselves from being moved. *Performance Research*, 20(5), 4–9.

Simon, Y. (2018). Emma Gonzalez going silent is the most powerful moment from March for Our Lives protest. http://remezcla.com/culture/emma-gonzalez-march-for-our-lives-moment-of-silence/.

Tognotti, C. (2018, 24 March). Transcript of Emma Gonzalez's March for Our Lives speech will absolutely crush you. *Bustle*. www.bustle.com/p/transcript-of-emma-gonzalezs-march-for-our-lives-speech-will-absolutely-crush-you-8596656.

Winterson, J. (2016, June 24). We need to build a new left. Labour means nothing today. *The Guardian*. www.theguardian.com/politics/2016/jun/24/we-need-to-build-a-new-left-labour-means-nothing-jeanette-winterson.

4

QUEERING *MX*

The self does not undergo modifications, it is itself a modification.
—(Deleuze 1968, p. 100)

Rooftop Tokyo

We are sitting on a roof terrace in the Shinjuku ward in Tokyo in the waning hours of a hot summer day. It's our first evening in this immortal city. The sounds and senses, as always when traveling, are overwhelming. The sun starts to set. The light becomes more orange, longer shadowed, and the breeze picks up, here on the 13th floor. High-rises surround us, geometric shapes more than buildings, economies or culture. The terrace is alive with sun-worshippers, a cross-section of young and beautiful Anglo and Asian affluents who seem perfectly at home with our boyish waiter who speaks a smattering of many languages, as so many must in this global economy.

The suns sinks like a jazz bassline. The young people drink heavily, their laughter carried up and over the terrace on the gusts of a humid breeze. They are well dressed, hip, in groups (none alone, of course). The men look like men, slim and well pressed; the women like women in cool fabrics and colorful shoes.

> They drink, they eat, they laugh.
> They are beautiful.
> They seem to have bottomless pockets, limitless energy, and borderless confidence.

> I look at her and I don't think words (highly unusual for a writer).
> I look across the table at her and the tears come to my eyes, my chest fills up.

I look around at the "beautiful people," the beautiful view, the incredible privilege that has brought us here, that buoys us above the water in the sea in which I drowned or barely survived, floating, for so so so many years.
What has made this so?
What has turned the tide toward this incredible affluence that I feel but can hardly recognize?
What has allowed me to break above the waves, rather than go down under them, like so very very many good people do?
What is the right way to live, when affluence comes?
What are the right commitments, when power and privilege comes?
How can we come together, how can we change things?
How can I not be seduced by this beautiful day, this moment, this light? This love?
It is everything, and it is terrifying.

I look across at her and my love for her explodes inside my chest.
I smile.
She looks up, feeling my gaze.
I smile, tears well in my eyes.
She reaches across a table, on the 13th floor of a hotel in Tokyo, and takes my hand.
We don't speak.
She smiles.
"It's just so—perfect," I say.
Everyone is happy. I am happy and I don't feel guilty for it.
I am happy and I'm not alone.
I'm not alone.
I have always been alone.
How did this happen?

Shinjuku Calling

Six months later, we sit in the National Gallery of Victoria in Melbourne studying Yamagami Yukihiro's installation *Shinjuku Calling*, 2014 (NGV 2018). We are called back to Tokyo, to the buzz and press of Shinjuku and to the heat, the beauty and the giddiness of our stay there. Yukihiro's work assembles and disperses, the day dawning and waning in front of us. The installation is in two parts: there's an underlying structure formed by a meticulous pencil drawing of the streetscape in front of Shinjuku station—the busiest train station in the world. Graphite lines form the tracks, pedestrian crossings, buildings and screens. The second part is a video projected onto the drawing showing the movements of pedestrians, passing trains and cars, sun and clouds, of time itself. City lights and images play across huge video screens once the sun goes down. The still and silent streetscape is punctuated with ghostly bursts of movement, goes silent, then roars back to life with the arrival of the trains and people, with the passing of the day.

Shinjuku itself is a composite of forces, contradictions and the pulse of time—home to some of Tokyo's tallest buildings and government offices, the lush and cool Shinjuku Gyoen, a blend of Japanese, English and French formal gardens and the Golden Gai, a series of cramped alleyways home to themed clubs and bars able to host only three or four patrons at a time. Shinjuku is also home to the gay district Ni-chome, formerly one of Tokyo's most vibrant red-light districts, now populated by a skyscape of billboards featuring glittery, pop-star images of an array of non-binary young people who beckon to the passersby streaming below. The street-level structure of sex trade, homophobia, resistance and voyeurism dances with neon projections of genderqueer glamor and all manner of kei, or specialized pleasures, mingling and blurring them to the pulse of changing light and color. Shinjuku calling: a proliferation of codes as the vital movement of time, gender, pleasure and affect. Shinjuku calling: queering *Mx*.

★

There is a growing body of scholarly literature about non-binary gender identifications, not only moving beyond the simple 'trans' identification which returns always to the Mr./Ms. binary (Apter 2017; Hord 2016; Richards et al. 2016; Yavuz 2016), but now strongly moving toward a more nuanced and diverse field of gender representations (or resistances). Perhaps the most evident is '*Mx*,' a gender-neutral if not gender-resistant pronoun identifier (depending on whom you ask) (see for example Rosman 2015; Stotko & Troyer 2007; Pullum 2012). Popular publications have been helping folks understand how to say it, and what it means, for nearly ten years now, but in formal (like work) settings and institutional (like census) settings, *Mx* has still a long way to go. *Time* magazine defined it in 2015 as:

> If you don't feel like labeling yourself a Mr. or a Ms. and would rather leave your gender unknown or undeclared, *Mx*. (pronounced like *mix*) is a gender-neutral option. . . . Dating back to at least the late 1970s, the *M* was taken from the first letters of those gendered honorifics, and the *x* was attached to suggest an unknown quantity or thing, like it might in algebra class . . . One might use the honorific because they identify as bigender (having two genders), agender (having no gender), gender fluid (experiencing gender in different ways at different times) or perhaps just because they don't feel like their gender is a defining part of who they are, which needs to be staked out for all to see right in front of their name. *Mx*. could also be used when referring to a transgender person whose preferred pronouns (he or she, him or her) aren't clear.
>
> *(Steinmetz 2015, n.p.)*

Mx, like its antecedents and accompaniments *zhe, zie, ze, zir, hir* (Feinberg 1998), has a long history as a signifier resisting and rejecting heteronormative identifiers and is an important part of a *history* of feminist activism (Mallinson 2017, p. 432). The adoption and use of *Mx* is an act of *transcoding*—a term borrowed from digital media scholar Lev Manovich (2001) to name the movement from one form of coded language to another in a process of "cultural reconceptualization" (p. 47). He writes, "to transcode something is to translate it into another format" (p. 47). The process of transcoding involves the substitution of cultural categories and concepts with new categories and concepts derived from the "computer's ontology, epistemology and pragmatics" (p. 46).[1] In other words, the changes in language and meaning affected through the 'logics' of computer technology in turn influence, shape and change the 'logics' of culture. Culture and technology are 'composited' together. The same might be said of *Mx*, which substitutes and transcodes fixed and binary and singular categories and concepts with dynamic and multiplicitous ontologies, epistemologies and practices. Here, the *Mx* signifier marks a move from binary to non-binary gender identifications, paralleling the progression of computer coding from binary language to non-binary and non-human-driven mapping. Innovations such as OOP (object-oriented programming) move away from the traditional coding binary of "if . . . then" and toward more open-ended, complex possibilities of artificial intelligence (AI), mixed reality (MR) and virtual reality (VR). *Mx* can also be considered a nonconformist or resistant identification that offers a new and important strategy (or category of strategies) that 'queers,' in a particular kind of way, autoethnography.

Aliveness Engine

I can smell the alcohol and the bar food. I can smell the street drifting up from the alleyways below, reminding me that this is both a modern and an ancient city. Temporality is on display here. It is the past and the present all at once.

> It is the future and the past, all at once; the "future-past" (Manning 2009, p. 201).
> I can admit it: I'm the past.
> I can recognize it: these young people are the future.
> They are more mobile, wealthier and more confident than I ever had to be.

They are simultaneously more fluid and more fixed in their gender, their sexuality, their subjectivities that I ever had, or wanted, to be.

The wind blows; the traffic whirs below. Katy Perry's voice streams through the speakers while the clientele speak a panoply of languages—Japanese, German, French, English, Hindi. The cigarettes, the alcohol, the food, the company—all of it a blend of western, European and Asian smells, flavors and sights, signifiers of mobility, power and choice. In the rooftop world above the city swirling below, we are a composite of cosmopolitanism. Or so it seems.

The breeze announces a shift from today's pressing humidity. The air smells like rain might be coming.

★

There are some moments when you can feel so hard it's like taste, like hearing, like touch—the gathering of the air, the quickening, the energetic pulses around you coalescing in a particular way. You know this moment will never come again. In fact, of course, no moments will ever come again, but this feeling of elongation or time-breaking is what Brian Massumi has called "animateness untethered" or "vitality affect" (p. 146). I am here. I am here in this place, at this time, with every cell and fiber vibrating connection across spacetime, a 'sensing body in movement' (Manning 2009). This is a liveness that goes beyond perception.

Walter Benjamin explored aliveness in relation to art (1996a, 1996b), but here Massumi (2011) turns to its relational quality (p. 146) and readiness potential—how "movement can be felt before it actualizes" (Manning 2009, p. 146). This sense of aliveness is both part of our senses—we can see the people around us, we can hear the sounds, we can feel the sensations, we can smell everything—and also a kind of extra-awareness: we feel our accelerating response, the gathering of our own readiness potential, moving beyond abstractions of beauty or perception to the ways in which "the body is capacitated" (p. 43) by the abstraction and symbolism in art.

Artworks are privileged sites where, in the reflection and representation (indeed substitution) of *a* or *the* world, a "semblance of truth takes place" (Koepnick 1999, p. 38). Truth in artworks unlinks the logics and regulative forms of reasoning in theoretical knowledge, resides in moments of "discontinuity" and resists closure (Koepnick 1999 p. 38). *Semblance* relies on the origins of the word as noun, an outward appearance, and semble as verb, to bring together, in the German *schein*, or the kind of 'coming alive' as the illumination or emanation of 'appearance' in a work of art. Benjamin's semblance goes beyond appearance, observation or identification and into a gathering toward agency in the body that perceives it.

Massumi (2011) borrows from Daniel Stern (1985, pp. 53–61; Stern 2010) in using vitality affect to describe this sense of perceptual *wide-awakeness* (also developed, albeit differently, by Maxine Greene 1977). "We don't just look, we sense ourselves alive . . . The form naturally poises the body for a certain set of potentials" (Massumi 2011, p. 43). Massumi (2011) defines semblance as "another way of saying the experience of a virtual reality," where that virtual is the "abstract event potential" and semblance is "the manner in which the virtual actually appears . . . as lived abstraction" (pp. 15–16). Semblance is a kind of "thinking-feeling," in the way that the

> immediacy of the feeling isn't separable from abstractness, from the abstractness of potential, and from the semblance as the event's uncanny

self-abstraction, none of that can be parsed out into separate sense inputs . . . The hearing and the seeing wrap up together in the semblance.

(Massumi 2017, pp. 86–87)

In other words, there is a dynamism and an interdependent, agentic relationship between the observer and observed contained within Benjamin's (and Massumi's) conceptualization of semblance. In a word, there is a relational *force*.

This force—in art and other "aliveness engines"—gestures toward a something more beyond or behind the surface of appearance—a resonant "quivering" of experience that *moves* us. Benjamin calls this "beautiful semblance" (2002, p. 137). However, as the "beauty" in art is repeated, through form, it becomes not a semblance (in the sense of a gathering and gesturing beyond surfaces) but instead a *re*semblance (Massumi 2011, p. 177). In autoethnography, this formal resemblance is often described as the 'evocative,' though not in the sense of writing that "activates" feelings, subjectivities and visceral responses (Bochner & Ellis 2016, p. 61), which invokes the force of semblance. Instead, the 'evocative' in autoethnography is often used as a formalized form that we assume, if we recall and repeat it, will bring a kind of order and recognizability to the representation of experience. In other words, the 'evocative' in autoethnography "renders perceptible a hidden content in a formal resemblance" (Massumi p. 176). Resemblance strips the aliveness from art—and autoethnography—contenting it, organizing it, "deadening" it and resigning it to uncovering 'universal' truths through "first-person address"; the "exhortation" of this work is to personally identify, through resemblance (pp. 176–177). Massumi writes:

To identify, all you need is personal feeling and everybody human of any station presumably has that. Personal feeling: emotion. The universal reign of emotional generality claims the content of art, deadening the beautiful semblance and politicality of art.

(pp. 177–178)

What's needed in the face of this, according to Massumi and a host of other critical artists (Brecht 1964; Boal 1985; Barthes 1981; Butler 1997) is a means of "arresting" or "interrupting" the semblance of art and it's "trembling for truth," holding it still, and "spellbound" so that "the expression of truth hesitates, unable to complete the evocative retreat into the depths of reference. The a priori principle of resemblance waivers" (Massumi 2011, p. 179). He asks: "Might the suspension of the beautiful semblance give the expressionless legs? The better to world-line with? Does the quivering life struck with 'critical violence' bleed expanding life?" (p. 180).

Cruising Beauty

Queering autoethnography asks the same sorts of questions: Might the beautiful semblance of evocative autoethnographic representations be interrupted, or suspended by queering autoethnography? We have experienced and created work that does, indeed, give the expressionless legs and wrenches a more expansive existence out of the quivering postures of 'normal' life (Holman Jones & Harris 2017, 2016a, 2016b; Harris & Holman Jones 2017, 2016; see also Adams 2011; Adams & Holman Jones 2011, 2008; Alexander 2006; Fox 2013, 2010; Gingrich-Philbrook 2015, 2013, 2005; Harris et al. 2017; Holman Jones 2017, 2014, 2009; Holman Jones & Adams 2014, 2010a, 2010b; Johnson 2014a, 2014b).

★

We return to our room late, just as the rain begins to fall. You retreat to the bath, eager to wash away the heat of the day. I undress and pull on the blue striped cotton pajamas the hotel staff leave neatly folded next to the bed each morning. I am in love with these pajamas—in love with their fine cotton, their unisex style, their sharp lines. I have worn them every night and morning since we arrived. But not you. Despite their non-binary appearance and cool fabric, you say you feel constrained by their cut. By their press and certainty.

I sit in the window seat in front of the bed with the lights off, looking down into the wet street below.

The water pours from the tap, filling the tub.

Beautiful beings walk in twos and threes and fours. They wear colorful, body-hugging clothes, platform shoes, huge hats, parasols, feathers.

Heads thrown back with joyous laughter. Hands thrust into the air, beckoning.

You ease yourself into the water, exhaling in a long, pleasure-filled hum.

What I don't see or read or know is gender. These beautiful beings could be men or women, but they are not Mr. or Ms. or anything that distinct and stable.

Water laps over the sides of the bath, hitting the floor with a clap.

They are, instead, composites, their only unifying or certain characteristics are affective: they pulse, gather, intensify, disperse.

Water shifts and falls when you step from the tub.

The neon softens and shifts through the prism of the raindrops on the window, refracting and distilling the vibrant nightscape into a kaleidoscope of possibilities.

I turn when you open the door. You are outlined by the light and steam of the bath. You're wearing the blue striped cotton pajamas.

Sirens punctuate the hum of the street below.

Joyous laughter, rain. Beckoning hands. Sirens.

Outlined by light and steam, reflected in the prism of raindrops on the window, and the blue, blue crisp of hotel pajamas, you. And me. Beautiful beings, gathering, pulsing and intensifying with our own vibrant potential.

★

The queering of autoethnography signals the "something more" that might lie behind or beyond the surface of experience and because of this is an "aliveness engine" that moves us to consider how, even when the present isn't enough, there are "rich and riotous" futures just beneath, behind and beyond our perception (Halberstam 2011, p. 3). Muñoz (2009) describes queer futurities as what's "not yet here," noting that such futures "insist on another time and place that is simultaneously not yet here but able to be glimpsed in our horizon" (2009, p. 183). This is the readiness potential of queer autoethnography and other critical works in which futures—and the movements that accompany them and make them possible—can be felt before they actualize (Manning 2009). In this way, queer autoethnography motors the thinking-feeling needed to "cruise the fields of the visual and not so visual in an effort to see in the anticipatory illumination of the utopian" (Muñoz 2009, p. 18). Transcoding is also an aliveness engine for seeing and sensing the future, bringing the virtual into reality, though not in the sense of actualizing an alternative future in opposition to the here and now. Instead, the virtual as future is the quivering potential of the "physically not yet realized" aspects of human and embodied space (Draude 2015, p. 95). Both queer autoethnography and *Mx* transcode not only the language (and text) but also the meaning of gender in ways that respond to the aliveness of queer and trans★ subjectivities in the 21st century.

Body in Code

Manovich (2001) suggests that "new media in general can be thought of as consisting of two distinct layers—the 'culture layer' and the 'computer layer'"—in which the computer layer, like gender for Butler and other gender theorists,

> is not itself fixed but rather changes over time ... As hardware and software keep evolving and as the computer is used for new tasks and in new ways, this layer undergoes continuous transformation ... in summary, the computer layer and the culture layer influence each other. To use another concept from new media, we can say that they are being composited together. The result of this composite is a new computer culture—a blend of human and computer meanings, of traditional ways in which human culture modeled the world and the computer's own means of representing it.
>
> *(p. 46)*

Trans★ and genderqueer scholarship represents a rhizomatic proliferation of identity performances. The bodies of literature about coded bodies and bodies-who-code can be brought together around considerations of queer bodies' social functions as 'code,' a performative language that does and has always reflected dominant culture, in both its resistance to normativity as well as its patterning. There is, of course, the double entendre of the 'trans' in transcoding, one that we find a productive layering of worldings and spacetimes. In these worldings and space-times, the transcoding of the genderqueer body is a "body-in-code, a body whose embodiment is increasingly realized in conjunction with technics"

(Hansen 2006, p. 20). Such transcodings are, following Bruno Latour (1998), iconophilic—representations that emphasize movement "from one form to another, to the transformation, and the in-formation of the image itself: the body transcoded by technology" into the digital human and by art into aesthetic codes (Nayar 2007, p. 4). How then, to write, theorize and code "bodily ontology that protects, persists and flourishes" (Butler 2012) within the arresting event potential of the virtual as lived abstraction (Massumi 2011)? Such writing, as Massumi (2011) says, would deploy "an affective politics, more about seeding exploratory weather patterns than cultivating their determinant context, the particular ideas or behaviors that will be performed" (p. 68).

All the Luck and a Livable Life

Another night in the rooftop bar, two German boys drink and flirt at the table next to us. Their conversation lifts up and over the Taylor Swift song on the sound system and trickles down to where we are sitting. They are from different cities in Germany but talking about the kinds of different guys they have picked up recently, from around the world, a different kind of global mobility: A Brazilian guy who was funny and gorgeous but awful in bed, a Singaporean who was cruel. They talk about friends like themselves who, the guy from Berlin says, jumped out of an 11th floor window a few months ago. Life is hard, yet life is so much easier than it has ever been. How to make sense of it? How to make a livable life in the wake of these contradictions? How to go on?

The wall behind them says in neon: "It's good to unwind once in a while. We wish you all the luck."

We? We have all the luck. Where did all the luck come from, exactly, after so many years of no luck? Why do we get the luck, when so many never find it? So much hard work, so many missed chances, so much desire. So much persistence and so much failure. Yet here we are, prosperous and flush with love. We're grateful, and we feel the luck; it doesn't unwind, but rather twists, and tugs, pulling our bodies into attention and attunement. Into gratitude. Our eyes fill with tears as we look at each other across that table on the 13th floor of the Granbell Hotel, Tokyo. It's good to unwind, once, in a long, long while. Perhaps the question isn't how to make sense of it, but instead how to slow the process of sensemaking and representation "long enough to find ways of approaching the complex and uncertain" moments and world-lines "that "literally hit us or exert a pull on us" (Stewart 2007, p. 4). How to write it, the intensity of all the luck and the composition and compositing of a livable life?

★

Queerness is a particular kind of vitality affect, a form of aliveness, or wide-awakeness that assembles in difference and is practiced—both in failure and virtuosity—outside of normalizing temporalities and geographies (Muñoz 2009, p. 183). Queer affect takes on ineffable qualities in both temporal and online contexts and how we theorize, write and live queerly—autoethnographically and otherwise—requires a kind of transcoding from one form into another, where writing theory is a practice of writing code (Galloway & Thacker 2007) that strategically deploys the structures and logics of computer coding to write the "endless choices of queer non-essentialism" (Blas 2008).[2] And what of autoethnography as a compositing of first-person address, feeling and the virtual? Might this be a form of transcoding that goes beyond and beneath gender, and beyond and beneath resemblant depictions of self and other? Might the transcoding of/ by selves become a practice of queering both reflexivity and aliveness and in hybrid fleshed and virtual worlds? And how might such queering tremble with the wide-awake, "critical violence" of semblance rather than the mythic stability of normalizing social codes around gender and sexuality?

Judith Butler (2004) argues that stability of social codes around gender and sexuality are not helpful, possible or sustaining in terms of everyday lives. Butler's poetic argument about the necessary attention we must give to understanding what, in contemporary society constitutes a "livable" and thus "grievable" life also details what is not possible in its absence, in this case with regard to trans★ subjectivities and the diagnosis of gender dysphoria. Recognizing that so much has changed, regressed and thus remained the same since she wrote these lines, we quote Butler at length for the register and the cumulative power and aliveness of her words:

> The diagnosis of gender dysphoria requires that a life takes on a more or less definite shape over time; a gender can only be diagnosed if it meets the test of time. You have to show that you have wanted for a long time to live life as the other gender; it also requires that you prove that you have a practical and livable plan to live life for a long time as the other gender. The diagnosis, in this way, wants to establish that gender is a relatively permanent phenomenon . . . You would be ill-advised to say that you believe that the norms that govern what is a recognizable and livable life are changeable, and that within your lifetime, new cultural efforts were made to broaden those norms, so that people like yourself might well live within supportive communities as transsexual, and that it was precisely this shift in the public norms, and the presence of a supportive community, that allowed you to feel that transitioning had become possible and desirable. In this sense, you cannot explicitly subscribe to a view that changes in gendered experience follow upon changes in social norms, since that would not suffice to satisfy the Harry Benjamin standard rules for the care of gender identity disorder. Indeed, those rules presume, as does the GID diagnosis, that we all more or less "know" already what the norms for gender—"masculine" and "feminine"—are and that all we really need to do is figure out whether they are

being embodied in this instance or some other. But what if those terms no longer do the descriptive work that we need them to do? What if they only operate in unwieldy ways to describe the experience of gender that someone has? And if the norms for care and the measures for the diagnosis assume that we are permanently constituted in one way or another, what happens to gender as a mode of becoming? Are we stopped in time, made more regular and coherent than we necessarily want to be, when we submit to the norms in order to achieve the entitlements one needs, and the status one desires?

(2004, p. 81)

Elsewhere, Butler (2006, 2009) has written about the conditions under which we recognize lives as lives (and livable lives at that) and asks which lives are recognized as lost, as lose-able, and publicly mournable (Butler 2012, p. 11). She advocates a new bodily ontology that attends to the "rights of protection and entitlements to persistence and flourishing," noting that

to be a body is to be exposed to social crafting and form . . . in other words, the body is exposed to socially and politically articulated forces as well as to claims of sociality, including language, work and desire, that make possible the body's persisting and flourishing.

(p. 13)

For "subjects" and "lives" that are not quite or ever recognized as subject or lives, the social ontology of the body can and must and does "exceed the normative conditions of its recognizability" (p. 13). Butler is not suggesting that anybody (or subject or life) has, as its essential quality, a "resistance to normativity" (p. 13). In other words, queer subjects/lives or queering subjectivities such as *Mx* do not have an inbuilt predisposition towards difference, change or fluidity. And yet, the doing (or queering) of a livable life *does* exceed those normative conditions because of this, and requires time to do so (Butler 2012).

Where Butler rethinks the 'test of time' in gender expression as the building of a life that "requires time to do its job" (p. 13), we would like to rethink what it might mean to do—and live—research and scholarship that exceeds the normative conditions of its recognizability. The work of legitimizing ourselves within or against the 'norms' of the academy or meeting the 'test of time' turns us away from an autoethnography that is an active exercise of recognition of subjects and lives that matter/as mattering, even when they are deemed unrecognizable or ungrievable within dominant frames. Queering autoethnography makes these subjects and lives relevant, perhaps most powerfully through situating us essentially in "networks of being and of life that exceed us" by staging a "knowing encounter" between reader and author, the virtual and the real, the here and now and the not-yet that "does not quite know all that it knows" (Butler 2012, p. 13). Such encounters require time—to unwind and to take in both the persistence of failure and the flourishing of all the luck of privilege—to do their job.

A Bathhouse in Tokyo

We are boiling hot when we finally arrive at the onsen. We weren't sure whether we should go, worried about our gender expressions in the traditional space of a Japanese bathhouse, though our apprehensions about gender were superseded by other aspects of our embodiment at the first bathhouse we tried. It was a sleek, modern spa with calming music and fragrant bath salts permeating even the sidewalk out front. We went in, put our shoes away in the locker and made our way to the front counter, ready to spend megabucks for an afternoon in the cool water and mud baths. At check-in, the desk clerk asked us if we had any tattoos. I said yes first and showed her the very small infinity tattoo on the instep of my right foot. She said, "Oh no, I'm sorry, no tattoos." Tattoos are not allowed in most onsen in Japan due to their long-ago association with organized crime and the mafia. We made our case, noting that none of the tattoos on our bodies was large or even noticeable unless you were looking for them. All would be submerged in the onsen bathwater. She held firm. "I'm sorry, no tattoos." We reluctantly left, feeling dejected but determined to immerse ourselves in order to escape the July heat and humidity. We walked several blocks to the onsen in Koreatown because the clerk told us it was 'tattoo-friendly.' They took us and our tattoos, so we happily went in, paid and accepted the small hand towel provided.

We went—of course—into the women's side of the bathhouse. No choice there. No ambiguity, though there was one person in the locker room who looked like they might be trans★—muscular, hard jaw, cropped hair. I started wondering—where could I hide here? This is a strictly *nude* bathhouse—so where could a dick be tucked, in here? Where could a vagina or breasts be obscured, on the men's side? I love the women's energy, the old and young and variously shaped bodies. I love being able to go in there with my female lover, a privilege I will lose if I transition. I love being in a feminist space, in the second-wave feminist meaning—a place where only women go, where it's 'safe' to be whatever we want. But then:

That fantasy and bucolic feminist imaginary was shattered by the elderly "mother"-type female bathers who want to tell me where to go, when to swap hot/warm/cold pools, how to splash the cold water on myself. Just when I am trying to ease into the *freezing* bath, one of them feels compelled to splash me with her ice cold water. Perhaps she is trying to be nice, but she doesn't smile. Next she tells me that if I do not wish to do it her way, I should at least splash my rinsing water out into the 'public area' rather than the cold bath. I move away. I sit in the hot, hot, *boiling hot* bath, and wonder about power dynamics and the way they are so easily gendered. 'Men' do this, 'women' do that. I feel completely incapable of standing up to that woman. I do not speak Korean or Japanese so I'm at a disadvantage. I am, after all, in her country, in her space, inside her Saturday bath ritual. I don't want to insist, so I just move away. But is that fair? I have paid my money same as she has.

This very familiar yet queer interpersonal interaction makes me consider my genderfluidity: because I still have visible breasts and a vagina, I can enter this space. I can share it with my lover. What if I'd had top surgery? What if I'd come with a dick? What if I'd wanted to use the men's baths? If any of these things had been true, we would not have been able to have this brilliant restorative bathhouse experience together today, our last day in Tokyo. Sometimes I yearn to be in a non-female body but to remain in this female space, this familiar (if sometimes annoying) feminist space, relaxing with my female partner. As a feminist and a lesbian, I understand and appreciate 'women only' spaces. And yet, as a genderqueer and trans★-identified person, I feel uncomfortable and disappointed at the constraints of these binary alienations. Isn't it ever possible—ever, even now—to be to be an androgynous, gender fluid person with maybe breasts, a dick, a vagina, maybe no genitals, and a gloriously ambiguous presentation? I sink down into the lukewarm water and consider this beautiful, yet still elusive, chimera.

★

The transcoding of the queer body extends to our autoethnographic representations. As queer autoethnographers, our life is our work and our work a way of not only living, but also creating a livable life and a livable community.[3] In our collaborative lives, we are a genderqueer performance, moving together into and through the particularities of our bodies in a repeated performance of thinking-feeling, moving-mattering that persists, even in its discontinuity, in and through time. And in this work, we wonder how transcoding and the repetition of fluidity or gender nonconformity might challenge culture more generally, in the same way that queer challenges autoethnography? Gilles Deleuze (1968) unpacks the relationship between repetition and difference as an act, an ontological intervention into everyday actions. He contrasts the specific to the general, and insists that everyday lives are made up of specific repetitions, rather than vague generalities. These repeated specificities are too what constitute—in aggregate—a kind of transcoding of the queer body.

Following Deleuze, we embody a philosophical and transparently and importantly sexed and gendered history in which our co-writing is a textual and embodied performance of difference, offering an embodied ontological intervention into everyday actions (including scholarly work). In other words, our lives themselves are an affective engine for queering autoethnography.

Butler (1990) suggested more acutely than did those before her that rather than being *constructed* by a repetition of performed moments or acts, the most interesting thing about gender as performance is its openness to and cultivation of disruption. Elin Diamond, for example, argues that performativity is a reiteration of gendered codes so practiced and rehearsed as to become almost invisible (1996, p. 5). However, repetition in Deleuze's sense operates as both "repetition of the Same" and inclusion of difference in "heterogeneity of '*a-presentation*'" (1968, p. 24, emphasis ours). In other words, there are two kinds of repetition, "the static, 'reterritorializing' or repetition-as-representation; and the dynamic 'deterritorializing' of repetition with a difference" (Nealon 1998, p. 119). The work of gender transcoding that is *Mx* is the deterritorializing work of a-presentation that marks and includes gender difference and uncertainty and fluidity, rather than effacing it. *Mx* inhabits a traditional and accepted form of gender "in order to transform it from within, deterritorialize it" (Deleuze & Guattari 1987, p. 349). Similarly, the queering of autoethnography is a repetition with a difference; an a-presentation arrests and interrupts the trembling semblance of evocative personal storytelling (rather than resemblance of form or repetition-as-representation) from within.

Our tools of gender nonconformity (in-embodiment-in-writing) perform themselves as "willful subjects" (Ahmed 2014), extensions of ourselves, as collaborators, props, prosthetics. They play important roles in a queer transcoding of what Herbert Blau has called an "impasse in the quest of eyes" (1996), a cultural move toward *seeing differently*. Blau says,

> In my view, or viewfinder, there are those who can see and those who can't. And while I'm prepared to believe that what they see or choose to see may occur within a system of representation that tends to reproduce its power, there are also those who see so profoundly deep or so thick and fast—with such flat-out vision, in short—that it seems at times that the codes are merely catching up, while signifying practices are in their self-conscious transgressions suffering in comparison a semiotic arrest.
>
> *(Blau 1996, p. 193)*

In our queer a-performances, we play repetitively with this quest of the eyes, writing to see with flat-out vision; with deep thick fast code-switching transgressions. We write to see ourselves differently—to see the queer selves we transcode as *themselves* modifications of habituated and attenuated gender performances. In this work, we are only what we have (Deleuze 1968, p. 100)[4]; autoethnographic worldings that vibrate with difference beneath, behind and between becomings.

Bullet Train, Transcoding Community

We walk to Shinjuku Station to get the Shinkansen bullet train to Kyoto. The sleek train glides to a stop at the platform and we board. Inside, the train looks like it could be any regional train. Inside, you don't feel the 250 km/h speed. Things are still—suspended—even though you are tearing through the air. Outside, trees and people and towns whir past us in a blur. We press our phones to the window, taking videos of our journey. The sounds of trees and people and towns whirring past become a steady rhythm, *zhoom zhoom zhoom*. We watch videos of the bullet train from Tokyo to Kyoto on our phones. We are inside and outside, here and there, live and virtual. We are the rhythms and repetitions of movement.

When we arrive in Kyoto, we board another, slower train, and ride the short distance to the place where we can walk into a vast bamboo forest. The air is thick and wet. The forest is at once fecund and stifling. Above, the bamboo rises all around us, engulfing us, holding heat and the smell of earth over our heads. We crane our necks. Bamboo blocks out the light. Below, our feet are slick with mud and leaves. Mosquitos dance around our ankles. Sweat beads and falls from our eyelashes and fingertips. People everywhere, but somehow we are alone in this forest. We hold hands and look into the bamboo sky. We listen. Birdsong cuts through the heat, lyric and insistent. We reach again for our phones and hold them up above our heads, trying to catch the sound. A recording for our friend Craig, who makes beautifully queer soundscapes as a prelude and backbeat to the beautifully queer stories he writes-conjures-embodies-grows-lives. We wonder what kinds of stories will fall from Craig's fingertips as he sits perched in his Makanda, Illinois, study, looking out at the there-birds and trees as he listens to the here-birds and bamboo in Kyoto, Japan.[5] We three are here and there, above and below, live and virtual.

The train speeds back toward Tokyo in the dark. Outside, light hits and shoots across the windows, leaving behind an aura of color and energy. Inside, we sit next to each other, fingers tapping out a rhythm on keys. It is a deep comfort, writing when traveling. We are inside the habit, the gentle repetition and resistance of the words spreading onto the screen. Inside the wide-awakeness and readiness potential contained in movement into new spaces. The gathering and compositing of both.

We are recording and imagining and writing the quivering potential of experience, not only our own and not only now, but in the imagined spacetime of a queer community in code, a community "whose embodiment is increasingly realized in conjunction with techniques" (Hansen 2006).

We are there/then, in the bullet train from Kyoto to Tokyo and we are here/now, in the words on this page in the story of us.

We are transcoding gender and autoethnography, writing a flat-out vision that constructs more than livable lives and communities through the affective politics of queer.

Notes

1 For Manovich (2001), there are five principles of new media that are shaping the logic of how new media is understood and that are influencing its further development. His five building blocks of media ecologies are *numerical presentation*; *modularity*; *automation*; *variability* and *transcoding*. Looked at through a digital materialism lens, according to Van Looy (2003), these five key technical trends have 'assumed the role of cultural categories,' and in doing so point toward the social function of new media theory and practice in ways that inform queer bodies and assemblages. We extend Manovich's heuristic to

recognize the ways in which new media is not only changing the 'traditional cultural logic of media' in ways that create a composite "new computer culture blend: blend of human and computer meanings" (Manovich 2001, p. 63), but that create new kinds of postgendered cultural logics and human/posthuman subjectivities as well.

2   Blas (2008) characterizes such projects as "rhetorical" transcoding, noting: "The way policy makers and development experts translate the term *gender mainstreaming* into policy documents should be a crucial concern for feminist rhetoricians because this act of translation demonstrates how arguments shift and change due to economic and geopolitical contexts and thus shows how power informs rhetorics. . . . While the term *transcoding* describes the practice of translating digital data so that it works in several platforms, Inderpal Grewal [Yale feminist cultural theorist] has adopted the term *transcode* to describe how neoliberal logics (and I would add rhetorics) travel along transnational networks, subtly shifting and changing to fit various situations while seemingly maintaining a common ideology. Following Grewal's reification of the term and its original meaning, to change data while keeping to the data's integrity, I use rhetorical transcoding to mean 'the process of directly changing assembled code to work on different platforms'" (p. 31). We would characterize transcoding projects such as *Mx* and other efforts to change the 'data' around gendered subjectivities while keeping to that 'data's' integrity as queer(ing) transcoding.

3   Here we both reference Nick Trujillo's mantra that ethnography is a "way of life" and the echoing of this sentiment by Bochner and Ellis (2016) that autoethnography is a way of life and of living (p. 61).

4   Deleuze (1968) describes these selves as "larval," noting, the "self, therefore, is by no means simple: it is not enough to relativize or pluralize the self, all the while retaining for it a simple attenuated form. Selves are larval subjects; the world of passive syntheses constitutes the system of a dissolved self. . . . The self does not undergo modifications, it is itself a modification—this term designating precisely the difference drawn. Finally, one is only what one *has*: here, being is formed or the passive self *is*, by having" (Deleuze 1968, p. 100).

5   We are referencing Clifford Geertz's (1988) construction of 'Being Here' and 'Being There' in anthropology (and thus ethnography and autoethnography), which he describes as the "imaginative construction of a common ground between the Written At and the Written About (who are nowadays . . . not infrequently the same people in a different frame of mind) (p. 144). We note Dwight Conquergood's long-ago (and still salient) critique of Geertz's construction of the asymmetrical power dynamics in ethnography, which after the "crisis of representation" in anthropology turned to viewing culture as "text" and "fieldwork-as-reading" (2002, p. 150). Instead of "listening, absorbing and standing in solidarity with the protest performances of the people," the ethnographer "stands above and behind the people and, uninvited, peers over their shoulders to read their texts, like an overseer or spy" (p. 150). Our work to queer autoethnography seeks to listen, absorb and stand in solidarity with other queer people and performances as they exist across time and space, in this case as they ping and sing in a kind of simultaneous call and response between, through and in a bamboo forest in Kyoto and the tree-dense surrounds of Makanda, Illinois. We perform the kind of integration and "emotional texturing of theory" that Spry (2001) equally long-ago suggested creates a "live participative embodied researcher" (p. 709; see also Spry 2016 for a continuation and extension of this argument). We build on these ideas in exploring the resonances that transcoding has for queering autoethnography and how writing after Blau's (1996) flat-out vision that breaks into—and moves behind, beneath and perhaps beyond—systems of representation that reproduce their own power and speeds like a bullet train between here-there and real-virtual so fast that it seems "at times the codes are merely catching up" (p. 193).

References

Adams, T.E. (2011). *Narrating the closet: An autoethnography of same-sex attraction.* Walnut Creek: Left Coast Press.

Adams, T.E. & Holman Jones, S. (2008). Autoethnography is queer. In Denzin, N.K., Lincoln, Y.S. & Smith, L.T., eds., *Handbook of critical and indigenous methodologies*, pp. 373–390. Thousand Oaks, CA: Sage.

Adams, T.E. & Holman Jones, S. (2011). Telling stories: Reflexivity, queer theory, and autoethnography. *Cultural Studies<->Critical Methodologies* 11(2), 108–116.

Ahmed, S. (2014). *Willful subjects.* Durham, NC and London: Duke University Press.

Alexander, B.K. (2006). *Performing black masculinity: Race, culture and queer identity.* Lanham MD: AltaMira Press.

Apter, E. (2017). Gender ontology, sexual difference, and differentiating sex: Malabou and Derrida. *philoSOPHIA*, 7(7), 109–124.

Barthes, R. (1981). *Camera lucida: Reflections on photography.* Trans. R. Howard. New York: Farrar, Straus & Giroux.

Benjamin, W. (1996a). Beauty and semblance. In Bullock, M. & Jennings, M.W., eds., *Walter Benjamin: Selected writings*, Vol. 1, 1913–1926, p. 283. Cambridge, MA: Harvard University Press.

Benjamin, W. (1996b). On semblance. In Bullock, M. & Jennings, M.W., eds., *Walter Benjamin: Selected writings*, Vol. 1, 1913–1926, pp. 223–225. Cambridge, MA: Harvard University Press.

Benjamin, W. (2002). The significance of the beautiful semblance. In Bullock, M. & Jennings, M.W., eds., *Walter Benjamin: Selected writings*, Vol. 3, 1935–1938, pp. 137–138. Cambridge, MA: Harvard University Press.

Blas, Z. (2008). *transCoder.* http://users.design.ucla.edu/~zblas/thesis_website/transcoder/transcoder.html

Blau, H. (1996). Flat-out vision. In Diamond, E., ed., *Performance and cultural politics*, pp. 177–193. New York: Routledge.

Boal, A. (1985). *Theatre of the oppressed.* New York: Theatre Communications Group.

Bochner, A. & Ellis, C. (2016). *Evocative autoethnography: Writing lives and telling stories.* New York and London: Routledge.

Brecht, B. (1964). *Brecht on theatre: The development of an aesthetic.* New York: Farrar, Straus & Giroux.

Butler, J. (1990). *Gender trouble: Feminism and the subversion of identity.* New York and London: Routledge.

Butler, J. (1997). *Excitable speech: A politics of the performative.* New York and London: Routledge.

Butler, J. (2004). *Undoing gender.* New York and London: Routledge.

Butler, J. (2006). *Precarious life: The powers of mourning and violence.* London: Verso.

Butler, J. (2009). *Frames of war: When is life grievable.* London: Verso.

Butler, J. (2012). On this occasion. In Faber, R. & Halewood, M., eds., *Butler on Whitehead: On the occasion*, pp. 3–18. Lanham, MD: Lexington Books.

Conquergood, D. (2002). Performance studies: Interventions and radical research. *The Drama Review* 46(2), 145–156.

Deleuze, G. (1968). *Difference and repetition.* London and New York: Continuum.

Deleuze, G. & Guattari, F. (1987). *A thousand plateaus: Capitalism and schizophrenia.* Minneapolis and London: University of Minnesota Press.

Diamond, E. (ed.) (1996). *Performance and cultural politics.* New York and London: Routledge.

Draude, C. (2015). *Computing bodies: Gender codes and anthropomorphic design at the human-computer interface.* Wiesbaden, Germany: Springer VS.

Feinberg, L. (1998). *Trans liberation: Beyond pink or blue.* Boston: Beacon Press.

Fox, R. (2010). Re-membering daddy: Autoethnographic reflections of my father and Alzheimer's disease. *Text and Performance Quarterly*, 30, 3–20.

Fox, R. (2013). 'Homo-work': Queering academic communication and communicating queer in academia. *Text and Performance Quarterly*, 33, 58–76.

Galloway, A.R. & Thacker, E. (2007). *The exploit: A theory of networks.* Minneapolis and London: The University of Minnesota Press.

Geertz, C. (1988). *Works and lives: The anthropologist as author.* Stanford, CA: Stanford University Press.

Gingrich-Philbrook, C. (2005). Autoethnography's family values: Easy access to compulsory experiences. *Text and Performance Quarterly*, 25(4), 297–314.

Gingrich-Philbrook, C. (2013). Evaluating (evaluations of) autoethnography. In Holman Jones, S. Adams, T.E. & Ellis, C., eds., *Handbook of autoethnography*, pp. 609–626. Walnut Creek: Left Coast Press.

Gingrich-Philbrook, C. (2015). On Dorian Street. In Chawla, D. & Holman Jones, S., eds., *Stories of home: Place, identity, exile*, pp. 199–214. Lanham, MD: Lexington Books.

Greene, M. (1977). Toward wide-awakeness: An argument for the arts and humanities in education. *Teachers College Record*, 79(1), 119–125.

Halberstam, J. (2011). *The queer art of failure.* Durham, NC and London: Duke University Press.

Hansen, M. (2006). *Bodies in code: Interfaces with digital media.* London: Routledge.

Harris, A. & Holman Jones, S. (2016). Genderfication. In Rodriquez, N.M., Martino, W.J., Ingre, J.C., & Brockenbrough, E., eds., *Critical concepts in queer studies and education: An international guide for the 21st century*, pp. 117–126. London: Palgrave Macmillan.

Harris, A. & Holman Jones, S. (2017). Feeling fear, feeling queer: The peril and potential of queer terror. *Qualitative Inquiry*, 23(7), 561–568.

Harris, A., Holman Jones, S., Faulkner, S. & Brook, E. (2017). *Queering families, schooling publics: Keywords.* New York and London: Routledge.

Holman Jones, S. (2009). Crimes against experience. *Cultural Studies <-> Critical Methodologies*, 9(5), 608–618.

Holman Jones, S. (2014). Always strange. In Wyatt, J. & Adams, T.E., eds., *Presence and absence, love and loss: Autoethnographies of parent-child communication*, pp. 13–21. Rotterdam, The Netherlands: Sense Publishing.

Holman Jones, S. (2017). Waiting for queer. *International Review of Qualitative Research*, 10(3), 256–262.

Holman Jones, S. & Adams, T.E. (2010a). Autoethnography and queer theory: Making possibilities. In Giardina, M. & Denzin, N.K., eds., *Qualitative inquiry and human rights*, pp. 136–157. Walnut Creek, CA: Left Coast Press.

Holman Jones, S. & Adams, T.E. (2010b). Autoethnography is a queer method. In Browne, K. & Nash, C., eds., *Queer methods and methodologies*, pp. 195–214. Burlington, VT: Ashgate.

Holman Jones, S. & Adams, T.E. (2014). Undoing the alphabet: A queer fugue on grief and forgiveness. *Cultural Studies <-> Critical Methodologies*, 14(2), 102–110.

Holman Jones, S. & Harris, A. (2016a). Monsters, desire, and the creatively queer body. *Continuum*, 30(5), 518–530.

Holman Jones, S. & Harris, A. (2016b). Traveling skin: A cartography of the body. *Liminalities*, 12(1). http://liminalities.net/12-1/skin.pdf

Holman Jones, S. & Harris, A. (2017). I am a monument. In Holman Jones, S. & Pruyn, M., eds., *Creative selves/creative cultures: Critical autoethnography, performance, and pedagogy*, pp. 113–130. New York: Palgrave Macmillan.

Hord, L. C. (2016). Bucking the linguistic binary: Gender neutral language in English, Swedish, French, and German. *Western Papers in Linguistics/Cahiers linguistiques de Western*, 3(1), 4.

Johnson, A. (2014a). Doing it: A rhetorical autoethnography of religious masturbation and identity negotiation. *Departures in Critical Qualitative Research*, 3(4), 366–388.

Johnson, A. (2014b). Confessions of a video vixen: My autocritography of sexuality, desire and memory. *Text and Performance Quarterly*, 34(2), 182–200.

Koepnick, L.P. (1999). *Walter Benjamin and the aesthetics of power*. Lincoln, NE and London: University of Nebraska Press.

Latour, B. (1998). How to be iconophilic in art, Science, and religion?. In Jones, C.A. & Galison, P., eds., *Picturing science, Producing art*, pp. 418–440. New York and London: Routledge.

Mallinson, C. (2017). Language and its everyday revolutionary potential: Feminist linguistic activism in the United States. In McCammon, H.J, Taylor, V., Reger, J, & Einwohner, R., eds., The Oxford handbook of U.S. women's social movement activism, pp. 419–439. New York: Oxford University Press.

Manning, E. (2009). *Relationscapes: Movement, art, philosophy*. Cambridge, MA and London: The MIT Press.

Manovich, L. (2001). *The Language of new media*. Cambridge, MA and London: The MIT Press.

Massumi, B. (2011). *Semblance and event: Activist philosophy and the occurrent arts*. Cambridge, MA and London: The MIT Press.

Massumi, B. (2017). *The principle of unrest: Activist philosophy in the expanded field*. London: Open Humanities Press.

Muñoz, J.E. (2009). *Cruising utopia: The then and there of queer futurity*. New York: New York University Press.

National Gallery of Victoria (NGV), Triennial Voices. (2018). *Yamagami Yukhiro/Japan*. www.ngv.vic.gov.au/triennial-voices/artists/?a=59

Nayar, P.K. (2007). The new monstrous: Digital bodies, genomic arts, and aesthetics. *Nebula*, 4(2), 1–19.

Nealon, J.T. (1998). *Alterity politics: Ethics and performative subjectivity*. Durham, NC and London: Duke University Press.

Pullum, G.K. (2012, April 13). Sweden's gender-neutral 3rd—person singular pronoun. *Language Log*. http://languagelog.ldc.upenn.edu/nll/?p=3898.

Richards, C. et al. (2016). 'Non-binary or genderqueer genders'. *International Review of Psychiatry*, 28(1), 95–102.

Rosman, K. (2015, 5 June). Me, myself, and *Mx. New York Times*. www.nytimes.com/2015/06/07/style/me-myself-and-*Mx*.html?smid=tw-share.

Spry, T. (2001). Performing ethnography: An embodied methodological praxis. *Qualitative Inquiry*, 7(6), 706–732.

Spry, T. (2016). *Autoethnography and the other: Unsettling power through utopian performatives*. Walnut Creek, CA: Left Coast Press.

Steinmetz, K. (2015, 11 November). This gender-neutral word could replace 'Mr.' and 'Ms.' *Time/Living*. http://time.com/4106718/what-*Mx*-means/

Stern, D. (1985). *The interpersonal world of the infant*. New York: Basic Books.

Stern, D. (2010). *Forms of vitality: Exploring dynamic experience in psychology, the arts, psychotherapy and development.* Oxford: Oxford University Press.

Stewart, K. (2007). *Ordinary affects.* Durham, NC and London: Duke University Press.

Stotko, E.M. & Troyer, M. (2007). A new gender-neutral pronoun in Baltimore, Maryland: A preliminary study. *American Speech*, 82(3), 262–279.

Van Looy, J. (2003, February). Digital Marx: Manovich's new language of media. *Image & Narrative.* www.imageandnarrative.be/inarchive/mediumtheory/janvanlooy.htm

Yavuz, C. (2016). Gender variance and educational psychology: Implications for practice. *Educational Psychology in Practice*, 32(4), 395–409.

5

QUEERING MONSTERS

> We need monsters and we need to recognize and celebrate our own monstrosities.
>
> —(Halberstam 1995)

It Would Be Nice

Just sayin.
It would be nice to fall in love with a woman and have the whole world smile on it.
Just sayin I'm tired of the sideways glances the epithets the
puttin-up-withs
the horror, the fear, the anger, the disappointment of parents—mine and hers.

Just sayin I wonder cuz I have never known what it's like to fall in love with a person and have your family shout it from the rooftops, throw a party, roast a pig
buy us a house
take us on holiday
lend some money to get on our feet,
register it at Macy's
pat us on the back,
give us away
love us for who we love
for who and what we are.

And you know I'm so tired of people sayin
no family's easy.
I don't get along with my in-laws either
that's what everyone gets.
Everybody goes through that.
No love is perfect.
No road is smooth.

Cuz some roads are smoother than others.
Cuz you don't know what it's like to hide your passion.
Always hiding or apologizing for our great loves.
It's a burden.
It's a soul-eating heart-wrenching
starting-on-the-back-foot ache in the guts.
It's not a small thing.

I'm so tired of compromise Go slow. Don't flaunt it.
So tired of that bullshit.
Is it so much to ask?
If it wasn't so complicated it wouldn't be a relationship status on
Facebook,
now would it?

Do we ever get our time?
Can our families and friends be glad for us, ever?
Or is it always hard, always compromised, always a little bit perverse?
Can our friends be a little less self-congratulatory that they have
celebrated a 'gay' union?
Can our families stop being so pleased with themselves that they've
moved beyond outright shunning? Be better than that.
It would be nice if the world would be better than that. Yes it would.

The Monster/ous Liminal Zone

Those of us within gender's 'liminal zone' exist somewhere outside of heteronormative relationships and institutions; we are not intelligible to friends and family and social others who move comfortably within normative relationships and institutions (Butler 2004, pp. 57–58). What does it mean to be unintelligible? It means that we are not seen or understood or treated as recognizably *human*; our lives are not valued or grieved *as lives* (Butler 2006, p. 146).

Even when queer[1] gender identifications and sexualities are visible in the mainstream, certain performances of gender and sexuality remain hidden, misunderstood, unseen and unseemly—in a word, *monstrous*. Think of Mary Shelley's *Frankenstein*,[2] a character and a story that have become shorthand for how some human beings shun, disregard and damage others, the monstrous as a construction—a figure who signifies selves and ways of living the world cannot "bear to see" (Butler 2014, p. 41). A liminal figure, *Frankenstein*'s monster—and the novel as a prototypical monstrous narrative—functions to:

> keep women in their place, and yet the monster may well be carrying that excess of gender that fails to fit properly into 'man' and 'woman' as conventionally defined. If the monster is really what a 'man' looks like when we consider his aggressive form, or if this is really what a 'woman' looks like when her own gendered place is destabilized . . . then the 'monster' functions as a liminal zone of gender, not merely the disavowed dimensions of manhood, but the unspeakable limits of femininity as well.
>
> *(Butler 2014, pp. 47–48)*

Unintelligible subjects such as genderqueer persons who resist binary definitions of gender and femme lesbians who often remain invisible but live heteronormatively noncompliant lives are persistently co-opted, condemned or cast out of heteronormative society. This is nothing new. Consider Virginia Woolf's words in 1929: "It is fatal to be a man or woman pure and simple; one must be woman-manly or man-womanly . . . some marriage of opposites has to be consummated" (p. 78).

And while careful and hard-won distinctions between gender and sexuality identifications have expanded what is 'intelligible' in diverse sociocultural contexts, queer genders and sexualities co-create, destabilize and sometimes obfuscate one another.[3] What does it mean, then, to move through the world as a creatively queer yet monstrously unintelligible subject, just at the time that the majoritarian 'civilized' world congratulates itself on finally 'understanding' LGBTIQ experience? In contemporary visual and social media culture, not being seen—being invisible—is itself a monstrous proposition. Scholarship into the historical invisibility of sexual diversities and non-binary gender experiences (Chesser 2009; Rimmerman & Wilcox 2007) and the rise and fall of queer vilification demonstrates the historical fragility of being visibly queer. We learned in the 1990s that at times silence does equal death; and even while we are here and we are queer, speaking has consequences, as Barthes laments: "The other is disfigured by his persistent silence. . . [but] I too am disfigured . . . Soliloquy makes me into a monster" (2002, p. 166).

Like Shelley and her monster, we look into the mirror and we wrestle with our desires, passions, places and lives in a society that demands repetition, reproducibility and above all intelligibility (Butler 2014, p. 42). We look into the mirror and make the invisible visible (Solnit 2014, p. 53) by making creatively queer expressions of non-binary trans★ gender subjectivities and femme gender expressions and sexualities intelligible. We continue the project of disrupting the heteronormative center in productively monstrous ways, not only in the now but in our efforts to creating "distinctly queer and alternative futures" (Halberstam 2011, p. 78).

And we write. We write ourselves as figures who move in and through a monstrous narrative as a "form of unleashing"—a way of writing ourselves out of the 'bind' of gender binaries, heteronormative desires and traditional forms of kinship (Butler 2014, p. 40). We write the power of being seen but not understood, of passing unnoticed, of subverting sexual and gender fixities by simply moving and speaking through human landscapes, like Frankenstein's monster (and like Mary Shelley) did. We don't ask why queer desires and embodiments continue to be seen, read and understood as monstrous; rather we reckon with monstrosity as a kind of creatively queer embodiment of gender, sexuality and desire. We repeat transgender scholar Susan Stryker's words that "Monsters, like angels, functioned as messengers and heralds of the extraordinary" (2006, p. 247), a mantra. In a sea of increasingly mundane and unseen queerness, we are messengers of that extraordinary.

Should've Known

"Take your clothes off and get under the covers."

"All of them?"

"Yes. When you are a married, you sleep naked."

"My parents don't."

"Mine do. C'mon."

Laura sits on one edge of my twin bed and begins undressing. I don't believe what she says, but Laura's parents seem happier and are kinder to each other than mine are. I walk around and sit on the opposite side, my back to her. I take off my sandals, my cotton t-shirt—the one with the pink and blue owl on the front, my favorite—my cut-off shorts and underwear. I reach behind me, pull up the sheet, and slide backwards under the covers.

Laura inches close to me and puts her hands on my shoulder, turning me towards her. Afternoon sunlight pours in through the window behind her head, distorting my vision. Laura's hands are cold on my hot skin.

"When you are married, you sleep naked and you kiss, like this."

Laura closes her eyes and puts her lips on mine. She smells of grass and honey. The room is humid with our breath and the heat of our bodies. I close my eyes and press my lips to hers. The afternoon becomes one long kiss that ends only and abruptly when my mother comes home from work and calls my name. Laura and I sit up and pull on our clothes in a fit of laughter. My mother throws open the door and we freeze, hair disheveled, the bed rumpled, stupid grins plastered on our faces.

"What's going on in here?"

More laughter. My mother stands, frozen, a hint of a smile playing on her lips. "Laura, your mother is looking for you. Better get on home."

Laura brushes past her and turns to flash me a grin before disappearing down the hallway.

My mother stares at me hard. "Dinner in a half hour. Straighten up this room before your father gets home."

Nearly thirty years later, when I call my mother to say that I'm in love with a woman and have left my husband, she is silent for several moments, then says she's not surprised. Says she would've guessed as much. Says that while I was a pretty, affable girl with a steady stream of boyfriends she always wondered about Laura and the afternoon she surprised us by coming home early. Says she should've known. Why hadn't I?

Because We're Family

Despite the assimilating wave of gay marriage and trans★ visibility, it seems that queer is in constant conversation with the monstrous fringe of town. Frankenstein's monster is moving, breathing, seeking embodiment of what (and who) families and society name 'ugly,' 'dangerous,' and 'perverse'—the monstrous qualities that give rise to queer policing and vilification even today (Stryker 2006). Queer communities may be wide and diverse, but those who believe that queerness is now comfortably and universally intelligible or mainstream need only notice the campaigns of conservative politicians; the rise of homonationalism and pinkwashing; the predatory trolling of trans★ and queer youth social media sites and accounts; and the persistent lack of legal, educational and institutional protections for queer lives worldwide to remember that queer people are still frequently stereotypes, outlaws or scapegoats in a heterosexist and cisgender-centric world.[4]

Sometimes queer bodies and desires and relationships are performed in a socially acceptable and thus intelligible manner: we are recognized and validated in our roles as wives, mothers, daughters, sisters and teachers. But queer subjects also perform bodies, desires and relationships that are less than intelligible, unacceptable, unspeakable: butch, femme, androgynous, polyamorous, trans★, and gender creative. These performances are inflected with and sometimes deflect the rage, shunning and fear that Shelley's famous monster laments: the unspeakable, the ugly, the terrifying. How we make love, show love and speak love is unseen or, when seen, is often misunderstood, shunned or co-opted by those around us, despite others' belief that now they 'get' and accept us because they watch *Modern Family* or *Orange Is the New Black*.

★

A message from my sister, after months of silence following the conversation with my mother and what we all should've known: "I feel that I need to tell you that no matter who you love

or how you choose to live
it has absolutely no reflection on the fact that I love you. And my niece.
That's what family is about."

This message after the rejection, the refusal, the shunning.
After I'd planned a trip with my daughter to visit
my sister and her husband and children.
We were going to meet at our parent's house.
We were going to be together, as sisters, as family
for the first time in a long time.

For the first time since our children, now almost teenagers, were toddlers.
For the first time since I'd come out—as queer, as an other sort of woman,
another kind of mother.
For the first time in a long time,
we were going to return to the place of family
all of us, together.

After the weeks of planning,
seconds after I'd booked the flights I couldn't afford
a new message from my sister saying she wasn't sure
we'd see each other after all.
Her husband wanted to cut their trip short
because he wanted to get back early.
Because he had things do to at home—mowing lawns and washing cars.

I pleaded with her to stay just one extra night—
one night instead of the three we'd planned—
so that we might see each other
so the kids could laugh and swim for a few hours
with their grown-up cousins.
She said only, over and over, "I'll ask my husband.
Let me ask my husband."

Still, when my daughter and I arrived
and my mother met us at the airport
I asked after my sister and her family
because we are, still, family, after all,
I was surprised. I was genuinely surprised
when my mother said,
"Oh, they left this morning."

They left this morning. Oh.
But I am not surprised by the reason: because I am uncertain,

my queer desire a monster that children should be protected from
my femininity, my mothering, my language, my touch, my attention
too much to see, know, or risk.
And my child's chance to know where and who her mother comes from,
to know my tribe?
A casualty of the quarantine.

Now, years later, a message from my sister
saying that she loves me, no matter what.
No matter who I love or how. No matter what kind of woman I am
becoming.
Because we are family.

Not Yet

Elizabeth and I work together at a large insurance company. She writes proce-
dures manuals and I work as a technical editor, reading and shaping her work. She
is ten years older than me, gregarious and friendly. She wears red lipstick and tight
black sweaters that compliment her dark hair and blue eyes. We become friends,
sharing meals and seeing movies on the weekends. We begin a book club with
several other women who work in our building. When I tell Elizabeth I want to
move out of the apartment I share with my boyfriend, she invites me to stay with
her until I can find a new rental. I pack a suitcase and a few boxes of books and
take them to Elizabeth's house. She makes up the couch in her living room. In
the mornings, Elizabeth makes us coffee and I squeeze orange juice. We listen to
the radio in the car on the way to work, singing along. Some nights we stay up
late talking on the couch; on others she invites me to lie on her bed and watch
television.

I look for an apartment of my own, but I don't see anything I like. I stay on
with Elizabeth for months and we develop a routine, hosting the book club in the
backyard, taking swing dance lessons together, and having dinner with a lesbian
couple from another department every Wednesday night. Our rituals are a relation
trying to nudge itself into being—to free itself, to learn to be itself, to lose itself
in a pattern we are already caught up in.[5]

Friends at work comment on how close we seem. When I say *yes*, they stare
back at me, blinking, not sure what comes next in the conversation. I wait. Smile.
Silence. Then these friends change the subject, asking me whether I'm seeing
someone—anyone—I like. They want to know if I've found someone—anyone—
companionable, attractive, suitable. Boyfriend material. And I want to say *yes*—I
have found someone I like. Someone companionable, attractive and suitable,
though not exactly boyfriend material, but I don't. Not to them, not to Elizabeth,
not to myself. Not yet.

Even then I knew that intelligibility of femme or feminine sexuality is still understood as only and always a sign of heteronormative erotic and relational desires, one that renders queer desires and relationships invisible or unintelligible (Shoemaker 2007, p. 322). The rejection of such embodiments and desires is evidence of the continued replication—without deviation—of a gendered and heteronormative binary, compulsory reproduction, and straight families (Hill Collins 1998). Shelley's *Frankenstein* reminds us that such replications "produce monstrosity as a matter of course" (Butler 2014, p. 43). The monster's search to belong demonstrates how:

> replications never turn out quite as we might expect, that there is something monstrous at the core of replication, and that the desire for the perfect copy of a perfected image [of gender, of heterosexual desire] is not only monstrous, but breeds forms of monstrosity that expose both the impossibility and the cruelty of such a demand.
>
> *(Butler 2014, p. 43)*

What Frankenstein and his monster wanted, most of all, was to find and make family—however impossible, however cruel—because family is *the* primary site of belonging and solidarity for individuals and by extension various (racial/ethnic, geographic, religious, etc.) groups, even as it serves as an uncontested proving ground for "psychological health, appropriate partnering and child rearing practices, social acceptability and general normative behaviour" (Peterson 2013, p. 486). Families are also one of the first places we learn to enact and shield ourselves against the normalizing violence of queer and transphobia, racism, misogyny and class warfare. The desire to belong to a tribe—to be held, to be protected and nurtured, to have our loves cherished and our losses mourned—is a powerful force that propels us down a path of acceptance paved with institutional and social support (Ahmed 2016, par. 39). Leaving or deviating from that path enacts a kind of fatalist break, a queer "self-shattering that consigns us to a miserable fate, queer as a death sentence" (Ahmed 2016, par. 36). And then if things "do shatter (as things tend to do), you have fulfilled an expectation that 'this' is where being queer led you to" (par. 36). Who or what is broken in this story? Who or what fails to hold itself together? And can a monstrous narrative explain how we—and this—came to be damaged in the first place (Ahmed 2016, par. 42)?

The Monster Is a Mirror

In the bathroom mirror,
I trace my adopted child's lips with my fifteen-year-old finger and wonder
what tribe I come from,

who has lips like mine, where did I get them from?
In another bathroom mirror thirty years later, I trace
my genderqueer lips with my forty-five year-old finger and
wonder how these girl lips and boy bits fit together.

Where did they come from? Who is like me?
Am I monstrous or beautiful, or both?
I've begged my god just like Shelley's monster did, for a
"creature . . . as hideous as myself; the gratification is small,
but it is all that I can receive, and it shall content me.
It is true, we shall be monsters, cut off from all the world;
but on that account
we shall be more attached to one another."[6]
And so we were, my monster/s and me.

Shunned and scorned by his creator, Frankenstein leaves his home, his 'family' in search of human others who will recognize him, love him, take him in. At every turn, his efforts are met with repulsion, horror and violence. None of this makes sense to the monster—none of it, that is, until he encounters his reflection in a clear pool of water. At first, he is unable to believe that he was seeing himself in the mirror, unable to recognize himself as one of the graceful, beautiful cottagers he has grown to love, of whose family he longs to be a part. Though if the monster is unrecognizable as a member of that human clan, it is his creator's refusal to face him—to know him and to claim him as his own—that convinces Frankenstein that he is the monster the world takes him to be.

If we, as Toni Cade Bambara says, "discover [ourselves] in the mirror," there is labor to be done in both the looking and the seeing (2015, p. xxxi). There is vulnerability in reflection, in standing before yourself, others, looking back. The refusal to engage with the self in the mirror—the selves we do not want to face, own, or know, is "dangerous, to that self and to others . . . Elaborate are the means to hide from yourself, the disassociations, projects, deceptions, forgettings, justifications and other tools to detour around the obstruction of unbearable reality" (Solnit 2014, pp. 52–53). For many gender creative and other queerly identified people, mirrors—like families—can be sites/sights of not only the painful work of seeing the self as a creation—an "unfinished becoming [that] only ends" when we do (Solnit 2014, p. 53), but also the sites/sights of betrayal and loss:

> In the mirror: I look but I do not know who I see. . . . I cannot discover myself in the mirror, for the mirror is a monster. Go to the mirror and smash it . . . I ask my psychoanalytically-oriented therapist: 'What is wrong with me?' There is nothing wrong with me, she says. It's the world. The world has gone mad. . . . What's the curiosity about anyway? Why is difference so

shocking? Why should we all look the same, why should we be gender-polarized? Difference should make a difference.

(Morris 2002, pp. 138–139)

The conversation with one's reflection is a conversation with the world. Asking the question, 'what's wrong with me?' turns outward and becomes 'what's wrong with the world?' Though the very criteria we use to judge genders and sexualities—the criteria that "posits coherent gender as a presumption of humanness"—are the criteria that govern our own assessments of ourselves, our own ability to "recognize ourselves at the level of feeling, desire and the body, at the moments before the mirror" (Butler 2004, p. 58).

What do we see when we stand before the mirror? The visibly invisible femme, the genderqueer body—the 'girl with a dick'—do reflect not a twisted, unintelligible identification or desire but instead show us how heterosexist gender and sexual difference is itself an *imaginary*, by promoting an alternative to that imaginary (Butler 1993, p. 91). And yet the queer body in the mirror, as Butler's discussion of the lesbian phallus[7] makes clear, does not "represent a body that is, as it were, before the mirror: the mirror . . . produces that body as its delirious effect—a delirium which we are compelled to live" (1993, p. 91). And the monster? The monster is a public mirror reflecting a desire for belonging and love that is "considered aversive and largely disavowed" Butler 2014, p. 38).[8] Where has queer pride in seeing ourselves in the mirror gone? Where too has our rage at the world gone?

The Likes of Which

While my mother lays motionless four floors up,
while her brain is being bathed in a creeping bleedout which
will wash her away from this red raw world,
My brother's and my lifetime feud bursts like a boil on the surface
of that bubbling cauldron of family not-family/love and hate/
a lifetime of unresolved abuse and anger and oppression, a web of not-
belonging, all festering into today:

Down for a cigarette in the hospital parking lot, we end up
ten feet apart
reaching for the closest weapons we can find:
"You're a bully!" I choke, "You always have been and you are still and
I don't have to take it anymore."
I doubt he even hears me, screaming his own rebuttal,
but he pauses long enough to bark at me:
"You just want to have a dick!"

There is a pause in the psychodrama.
"Is that the best you've got? Seriously?" I say,
sort of laughing, sort of crying, and I walk away.
I walk away I walk away.
Even in the hour of our death amen
the homophobia and genderphobia is never far from the lips
of family, friends, colleagues, lovers, strangers:
Always a ready weapon. Just there. At the hip, waiting to be drawn.
As if a woman with a dick is the worst thing you can be.
Can't even say it's an accusation.
I mean, even the truth hurts when it's said in grieving anger.
Cuts like a knife.
And even a dull knife cuts.

Shelley's monster said it best:
"I have love in me the likes of which you can scarcely
Imagine.
And rage the likes of which
you would not believe.
If I cannot satisfy the one,
I will indulge the other."
And that's exactly what we do in humanland.
Exactly what we do.

The desire to connect is what makes the monster relatable as 'human,' but as his alienation, his unintelligibility, grows, so too does his rage (Feinberg 1998, p. 26). We, too, embody unintelligibility in our genderqueer/femme desires for relationality, our telling of the monstrous performed at the edges of the shame, rage and the un/speakable. The late transgender activist Leslie Feinberg describes the cut and fear of sharing our monstrous selves and desires:

> We have all been wounded in the ways we negotiate sex and intimacy; we fear communicating our needs and desires. Greater freedom to conceive the limitless potential of human sexuality, without shame, is an important and necessary contribution to all of humanity. And we need more language than just feminine/masculine, straight/gay, either/or . . . We need to refocus on defending the diversity in the world that already exists, and creating room for even more possibilities.

(1998, p. 28)

The shunning of 'unintelligible' gender embodiments and queer desire by mainstream media and culture creates the shudder of familiar (and familial) rejection. As Feinberg (1998, 1996, 1993) and others (Ziv 2014; Stryker 2006; Plante &

Maurer 2010; Nestle 1992) have noted, gender signifying can be a 'release' to the subject, but such resistive significations remain monstrous to outside others. Further, not all gender nonconformists are trans★ or intelligible as binary-identified others. Not all femmes are invisible, but nor are they seen or understood as resistively occupying hetero'normality.' If genderqueer and femme subjects remain constitutively invisible—and therefore unrecognizable *as* queer in the public sphere—what does the exoticizing of butch, F2M or genderqueer identities or bodies do to or make of 'intelligibility'? Such embodiments have the power to betray the idea of legibility itself (Duggan & McHugh 1996, p. 155). Asserting the value of nonconforming selves and desires by the so-called monstrously queer may be able to re(con)figure the violence of scapegoating and shame of unintelligibility, but if so, for whom?

Not Your Monster

Presenting an intelligible narrative of the self, as Judith Butler (2005) reminds us, carries a double price—the cost of telling that narrative in socially acceptable ways, as well as the toll of telling, over and over, the story of how we came to be and continue to survive in the unforgiving landscape of the social (p. 135). Proud, fluid, perverse and politically angry narratives are 'too hard' for most listeners to see, hear or bear, where stories of 'queer shame' are accepted as relatable, sympathy-generating and therefore socially acceptable 'survival' narratives. Though too often even these acceptable stories are met with 'queer fatigue' from the heteronormative and cisgendered center.

Telling a story that narrates a monstrous, unintelligible, non-binarized or otherwise 'unfixed' subjectivity poses "the risk, if not the certainty, of a certain kind of death, the death of a subject who cannot, who can never, fully recuperate the conditions of its own emergence" (Butler 2005, p. 65). So we omit the expected pronoun or the 'we' as acts of self-care, to protect ourselves from rejection. Or we overshare, trying to explain ourselves to others who seem to offer the possibility of belonging, whose prurient interest in our sexual practices and desires, dysphorias and fluidities, passings and refusals too often crosses lines of bodily and psychic dis/comfort. Such bargains are dangerous gambles for the queer subject, as they were for Shelley's monster.

However, taking the gamble means killing a "fantasy of impossible mastery, and so a loss of what one never had" (Butler 2005, p. 65). Letting go of mastery and mourning the loss of something we never had becomes, instead, an invitation to persistently (re)tell the story of a queer self and queer promise of something more creatively gendered or sexed (Butler 2005, p. 65): stories that are proud, resistant and celebratory. Stories that are both a balm and a catalyst for change. What if we read Shelley's *Frankenstein* as a performative in which monstrosity itself becomes monstrous, a "living form of critique of family, heterosexuality" and gender (Butler 2005, p. 46)?

★

I'm a goat.
I'm a stubborn Capricorn goat,
a slow-and-steady goat, and sometimes
a scapegoat.

Some people find me brave, and some people find me scary.
Some like me to fight their battles, but resent me for my battle-ready
ways.
Masculine women, genderqueer women and butch women are read as
resistant, willful and angry before we even open our mouths, but—

I share my story to give myself a chance
in the social body of belonging. Butler says,
"the monster may well be
carrying that excess of gender that fails to fit properly
into 'man' and 'woman' as conventionally defined. . .
The 'monster' functions as a liminal zone of gender. . .
disavowed and unspeakable."[9]
Disavowed and unspeakable.

I hope that by sharing my story you will share your story,
but often you don't.
Sometimes my bare and broken strugglestory gives you power,
lets you exhale back into your containment,
your normalcy, and you use it as a weapon against me,
instead of inviting me in.
It's the monster's weakness: the compulsion to belong.

Not all queers stay alive in the face of banishment
but those of us who do are strong motherfuckers who know the power of
a story.
Story is what keeps us alive, so we tell it
tell it
tell it again.
To remember that we are survivors.
To remember how we came to be damaged.
To remember the stories, a map of scars on our skin.

The Creatively Queer Body

Skin is something universal one can count on, rest within, or is it? As Judith
Halberstam (1995) has written, the monstrosity of figures like Frankenstein's
creation is carried in the skin. Monstrosity itself is made manifest in the flesh

and bone surfaces that collide with the affective materiality of other bodies not built through modification and prosthetics. The monstrous body "becomes a layered body, a body of many surfaces laid one upon the other," a self and site/sight of terror (Halberstam 1995, pp. 1, 28). Our layered bodies—bodies of many surfaces—while of beauty and value to those who co-construct us intersubjectively—become for others a landscape of gendered and sexual fear, vilification and violence (Halberstam 1995, p. 30). And yet we know that monstrosity is not simply a matter of appearance. It is a warning of what might happen (Halberstam 1995, pp. 44–45)—not only if the body is imprisoned by its desires, but also a warning about what an undisciplined, unfettered and unruly body might want, desire, look like and become.

We embrace the creative reimaginations of postsexualism (Foucault 1990) and postgendered bodies (Haraway 1991), though we long for the recognition that gender fluid and sexually diverse subjects are living out the material performance of these abstractions every day. And some days are better than others. We long too for the day when our queer communities—which can and do hold the antiteleological line—can manage fluidity for more than a moment without the perpetual surrender to mainstreaming in the name of incremental gains. We hope for an unforeclosed politics, one that "holds space, safety, options and shuts no one out" (Clare 2010, pp. 464–465).

The question of intelligibility for the genderqueer and queer femme subject remains a layer of many surfaces; even as we become intelligible to ourselves, becoming intelligible to lovers, chosen families and families of origin is another kind of becoming altogether. Becoming intelligible in and recognized by the world is yet another threshold. Each kind of becoming requires us to take a *stand*—an "upright, wakeful, knowing stand"—in the face of being "besieged by what [we] disavow" (Butler 2005, p. 65). Each morning, we take a stand. We stand before the mirror and look. We stare back at our reflections, each blink of our eyes raising and lowering the shutter between invisibility and visibility. Rage and acceptance.

★

> He passed me on the running track and said,
> "What the hell is that?"
> but I just kept running.
> I'm used to running.
> It's the safest place to be.
>
> What *am* I, anyway?
> What a question.
> What a glorious wonderful question.
> A question I ask myself every day. A question that can raise the curtain on
> a peep show of possibilities. A question to remind us all of the limitless

possibilities we came in with and have been slowly leeching out ever since.

A question of love, of sex, of gender and of vision.

What *am* I, anyway, and who or what did I come from?

★

I know who my forefathers are, and they do not include Benjamin Franklin.

My forefathers include Gertrude Stein, and Leslie Feinberg,
and Peggy Shaw of my East Village coming-of-age.

Back then I went to the shows, I went to the parties, I did what I could to find my gendered and queer self a home but, you know, emergence can be incremental.

I could not look at them and see myself, I could not.

Peggy Shaw is a tall strong butch woman who has owned herself and shared herself over a lifetime,

Reminding everyone of the shifting shaft of light that we call gender and

The dangerous cost of masculinity in women still today.

She stood nearly alone as a boi-beacon,

A real strong and silent type, she was.

Not beckoning to the world, like Frankenstein's monster,
just hollering out to it.

Take me or leave me, she said.

Take me or leave me.

Peggy and Lois Weaver reigned supreme and I

I gawked at them like some kid watching Santa Claus at Macy's:
a little bit of awe mixed with a whole lot of suspicion. And fear. And emotion.

So much emotion.

The problem sometimes with emotion is it wells up in you but you still don't know what it is.

I watched Peggy and Lois do their butch-femme thing for a long time, for years, and yet I couldn't unclench and be part of that scene
in any emotional way,

like a tight-fisted bully hanging around the edges of belonging and trying to bash my way in. Like, well, the monster.

And like the monster, I ran.

I turned away from those forefathers like Peggy in an effort to turn away from myself. But it didn't work, it never works. That is not the way the world pushes us inevitably toward reconciliation and self-love, even if only in our hearts.

Living between genders is also about living between private and public, coloring outside the lines,
about too much feeling in a too-little feeling world.

I was long gone from East 4th Street and long gone from Peggy Shaw
by the time I realized I was butch, more than butch, more than girl, more than gay.
By the time I met my boi self. My monstrous self that I can't love enough now.
Got lots of self-loving time to make up for.
Nothing but time.

A Life Worth Living

The liminal zone of gender troubles the notion of "one complete passage" from disavowal and recognition because "there are many tunnels through the thicket" and we must make the journey over and over again (Clare 2010, p. 464). Still, on the other side of that passage, there "lives an openness that lets us slide into our bodies and makes space for persistent joy and comfort" (Clare 2010, p. 464). We celebrate the spaces and the thickets, the passage and the starting over, all worthy becomings. The shame and rage that haunt us have also taught us to practice self-care despite the sociocultural odds, to make chosen families in order to survive our damaging families of origin, and to love our bodies and desires fiercely, even as those beautiful bodies—as we—remain unintelligible to mainstream 'outsiders.' We reflect our bodies and our selves to one another in nurturing ways, transforming the abject and shunning by growing a kind of 'body love'—a love that "can wake us up in the morning, put us to bed at night, visit us as we are dressing to go out or just singing along to our favourite song" (Clare 2010, p. 464). The movements and moments of this love aren't planned or charted (Butler 2004, p. 210). They "just show up one day in the mirror . . . however these moments arrive, let us build a community that nurtures them" (Clare 2010, pp. 464–465). When they arrive, we continue to look at them—and ourselves—and see a body worth loving and a life worth living.

★

I was the girl who could be loved, because I made sure I was lovable.
I was the good girl, the sweet girl, the feminine girl.
I was the pretty girl, but pretty is as pretty does (Weaver, qtd. in Shoemaker 2007, p. 330).
I was the girl who found a suitable, acceptable boy, who seemed like a reason,

and we moved out of small town America and headed to somewhere a bit
more possible.

Still, I ended up hiding out at the edge of town,
drawing up inside myself, again and again, waiting, watching.
How long does a girl have to wait to get what she wants?
How long and how far does she have to travel to find the place of
crossing,
the proliferation of desires?
To be a good girl, a femme girl, and a queer girl at the same time?

It has taken me a lifetime to find my want
in a basket out back behind the shed.
A basket full of overripe fruit and hungry mouths.
That basket, that want cannot contain me.
So many failed attempts
So many hungry mouths sewn shut.
So many disappointments.
So much time to make up for.

So when I found the boygirlboi who could love me,
who I knew could love me right
I remembered what I wanted.
I remembered who I was, even when I am invisible without you next
to me,
bound to the binary by people on the train,
by colleagues at the Christmas party
by family who love me but won't see me,
unintelligible femme, monstrous other.
Now you see me now you don't?[10]
Now you *don't*.

The river of my love and my rage floods the earth.
I cannot not hold my tongue any longer.
I will not omit myself from the conversation.
I am not your reason, your excuse, your night terror.

Your tolerance of me despite my contagion
your wishing me happiness while denying my existence
Is not belonging, is not acceptance, is not family.
And pretending it is, torches me in your own image.
A monster, after all, is a creation, a made thing (Stryker 2006, 249).
A siren call; a warning.

Messengers of the Extraordinary

To 'recognize' has two meanings: to know again (from having encountered before); and to acknowledge, to validate. Finding recognition is for queers and monsters both a matter of opinion and opportunity (Harris 2015). While some crave it, others actively reject the possibility, and still others celebrate our 'freak-dom' (Morris 2002). Yet monsters know the danger of ignoring the crowd, the townsfolk who run at us with pitchforks, who have strength in familial numbers, who have a normative posse. We continue to critically and poetically interrogate a monstrous culture in which true gender and sexual difference remains not only unintelligible but also unwelcome, despite a global euphoria about the mainstreaming of LGBTIQ visibility and acceptance. Such moves toward acceptance, we argue, pivot on compliance and reinforcement of heteronormativity, allowing a cultural imperative of scapegoating and fear of who and what remains unintelligible. We celebrate those who are working toward articulating a gender-creative spectrum that grapples with the failure of language (Ehrensaft 2011; Meyer & Pullen Sansfacon 2014; Beemyn 2015; Rubano 2015; Hite 2002) and a narrowing of the queer agenda(s) so hard-won over the past five decades, and proudly celebrate the creatively queer rather than participate in reifying gay shame narratives.

As global cultures move toward greater hegemony overall, and notions of sexual and gender creativity/diversity are subsumed into these narrowing, mainstreaming impulses, where will the monstrous go? Will it shift to other parts of our queer communities? Will it, and we—like Frankenstein's monster—flee to the ends of the known world? How can we celebrate remaining outside of hetero- and gender-normative culture? Queer monsters must stop running. Must turn around. Must face those who would kill us, chase us out past the city walls. Must face ourselves in the dark mirror of others' shunning of us, remembering that gaze is a reflection of how we might redefine a life worth living (Stryker 2006, 250). We know that monsters can be more than scary, more than scapegoats, more than terrifying reflections in a clear, clear pool. Monsters can be spirit guides who take your hand when you're fearful and lead you to extraordinary places (Barad 2015). Monstrously queer warriors push on into the dark and unknown territories of our minds, bodies, dreams. We in our difference are messengers of the extraordinary, of the infinity of nature, not—as they would have us believe—the unnatural.

> In the shifting shaft of light we call gender,
> the motion of that light on the river of our desires,
> the risk and sweat of troubling binaries and pushing boundaries,
> we create queer of ways of living and loving and looking in the mirror
> that make us into artists[11] and not only monsters.

> Celebrating our power, our beauty, our right to live as we are.
> Giving each other shelter on an otherwise desolate horizon.[12]

Remembering change on the inside doesn't have to wait for change on the outside.

Knowing revolution begins with a single act, and ours is our queer self-love.

So much time, so much self-loving time to make up for

So much time to enjoy, lapping it up like light in water.[13]

Filling our skin to its very edges.

Notes

1 For the purposes of this text, we consider femme, genderqueer and trans★ subjectivities as creatively 'queer' embodiments of gender and sexuality. We understand that these are not always helpful or appropriate alliances, but we make those connections here in order to draw parallels between our different yet similar experiences of a monstrous unintelligibility.

2 We continue to find the generative potential in Shelley's Frankenstein narrative, as others do, especially for considerations of unintelligibility, outsiderness, belonging, monstrosity and embodiment. In this chapter we draw primarily on Judith Butler, Judith (Jack) Halberstam, Susan Stryker and Karen Barad who have all used Frankenstein in service to these discussions—sometimes building upon each other's work to do so (see particularly Barad's use of Stryker in Barad 2015).

3 We are working to hold the hard-won distinctions between gender and sexuality alongside Butler's now long-ago (1993) assertion that it is "unacceptable" to "separate radically forms of sexuality from the workings of gender norms. The relation between sexual practice and gender is surely not a structurally determined one, but the destabilizing of the heterosexual presumption of that very structuralism still requires a way to think the two in a dynamic relation to one another" (p. 239).

4 Indeed, as we write this, rights extended to trans★ persons in the US during the Obama administration have been systematically repealed or challenged by US President Donald Trump, including a "license to discriminate" that allows federal agencies and other government subsidiaries to discriminate against trans★ persons on the basis of religious freedoms, a memo instructing Department of Justice attorneys to take the legal position that federal law does not protect trans★ workers from discrimination, the Department of Health and Human Services announced a plan to roll back nondiscrimination provisions in the Affordable Care Act for trans★ people issued by the Department of Health and Human Services, repeal of legislation allowing trans★ youth in schools to use the bathrooms matching their chosen identities and to serve in the US military (National Center for Transgender Equality 2017). In 2016, 220 anti-LGBT bills were introduced through state legislative bodies and in the first six months of 2017, another 100 anti-LGBT bills were introduced (Miller 2017). Worldwide, seventy-six countries criminalize consensual, same-sex relations, with punishments including prison sentences, flogging and the death penalty (Human Rights Watch 2017).

5 Stewart (2007) writes that the "affective subject" is a "collection of trajectories and circuits" that we "inhabit as a pattern [we] find [ourselves] already caught up in (again and there's nothing [we] can do about it now . . . Out there on its own, it seeks out scenes and little worlds to nudge it into being. It wants to be somebody. It tries to lighten up, to free itself, to learn to be itself, to lose itself" (59).

6 Shelley (1869, p. 115).

7 Butler (1993) notes that the lesbian phallus is not the penis, writing that "what is needed is not a new body part, as it were, but a displacement of the hegemonic symbolic of (heterosexist) sexual difference and the critical release of alternative imaginary schemas for constituting sites of erotogenic pleasure" (p. 91).

8 This is a rephrasing of Butler (2014), who writes: "After all, the monster is not precisely a mirror, but rather the articulation of desire considered aversive and largely disavowed" (p. 38).
9 Butler (2014), pp. 47–48.
10 Shoemaker (2007), pp. 324–325.
11 Solnit (2014), p. 53.
12 Shelley (1869), p. 83.
13 Delaney (2004).

References

Ahmed, S. (2016, 26 January). Feminism and fragility. *Feminist killjoys*. https://feministkill-joys.com/2016/01/26/feminism-and-fragility/.

Bambara, T.C. (2015). Foreword to the first edition, 1981. In Moraga, C. & Anzaldua, G., eds., *This bridge called my back: Writings by radical women of color* (4th edition), pp. xxix–xxxii. Albany, NY: SUNY Press.

Barad, K. (2015). Transmaterialities: Trans★/matter/realities and queer political imaginings. *GLQ: A Journal of Lesbian and Gay Studies*, 21(2–3), 387–422. DOI 10.1215/10642684–2843239.

Barthes, R. (2002). *A lovers discourse: Fragments*. London: Vintage/Random House.

Beemyn, G. (2015). Raising and empowering LGBTQ and gender-nonconforming youth. *TSQ: Transgender Studies Quarterly*, 720–724.

Butler, J. (1993). *Bodies that matter: On the discursive limits of 'sex'*. New York: Routledge.

Butler, J. (2004). *Undoing gender*. New York: Routledge.

Butler, J. (2005). *Giving an account of oneself*. New York: Fordham University Press.

Butler, J. (2006). *Precarious life*. London: Verso.

Butler, J. (2014). Afterword. Animating autobiography: Barbara Johnson and Mary Shelley's monster. In Johnson, B., ed., *A life with Mary Shelley,* pp. 37–50. Palo Alto, CA: Stanford University Press.

Chesser, L. (2009). Transgender-approximate, lesbian-like, and genderqueer: Writing about Edward De Lacy Evans. *Journal of Lesbian Studies*, 13(4), 373–394.

Clare, E. (2010). Resisting shame: Making our bodies home. *Seattle Journal for Social Justice*, 8, 2. http://digitalcommons.law.seattleu.edu/sjsj/vol8/iss2/2.

Delaney, S.R. (2004). *The motion of light in water: Sex and science fiction writing in the East village*. Minneapolis: University of Minnesota Press.

Duggan, L. & McHugh, K. (1996). A fem(me)inist manifesto. *Women and Performance*, 8, 2, 153–159.

Ehrensaft, D. (2011). *Gender born, gender made: Raising healthy, gender-nonconforming children*. New York: The Experiment.

Feinberg, L. (1993). *Stone butch blues: A novel*. New York: Alyson Books.

Feinberg, L. (1996). *Transgender warriors*. Boston: Beacon Press.

Feinberg, L. (1998). *Trans liberation: Beyond pink or blue*. Boston: Beacon Press.

Foucault, M. (1990). *The history of sexuality, volume 1 (an introduction)*. New York: Vintage.

Halberstam, J. (1995). *Skin shows: Gothic horror and the technology of monsters*. Durham, NC: Duke University Press.

Halberstam, J. (2011). *The queer art of failure*. Durham, NC: Duke University Press.

Haraway, D. (1991). A cyborg manifesto: Science, technology, and socialist-feminism in the late twentieth century. In *Simians, cyborgs and women: The reinvention of nature*, pp. 149–181. New York: Routledge.

Harris, A. (2015). A kind of hush: Adoptee diasporas and the impossibility of home. In Devika Chawla & Stacy Holman Jones, eds., *Storying home: Place, identity, and exile*, New York: Lexington Books.

Hill Collins, P. (1998). It's all in the family: Intersections of gender, race, and nation. *Hypatia*, 13(3), 62–82.

Hite, M. (2002). Inventing gender: Creative writing and critical agency. In Shumway, D.R. & Dionne, C., eds., *Disciplining English: Alternative histories, critical perspectives*, pp. 147–158. Albany: State University of New York.

Human Rights Watch. (2017). #Outlawed. https://lgbt-rights-hrw.silk.co.

Meyer, E.J. & Pullen Sansfacon, A. (2014). *Supporting transgender and gender creative youth*. New York: Peter Lang.

Miller, S. (2017, 1 June). Onslaught of anti-LGBT bills in 2017 has activists 'playing defense.' *USA Today*. www.usatoday.com/story/news/nation/2017/06/01/onslaught-anti-lgbt-bills-2017/102110520/.

Morris, M. (2002). Young man Popkin: A queer dystopia. In Anzaldua, G. & Keating, A., eds., *This bridge we call home*, pp. 138–139. New York: Routledge.

National Center for Transgender Equality. (2017). Trumps' record of action against transgender people. https://transequality.org/the-discrimination-administration.

Nestle, J. (ed.) (1992). *The persistent desire: A femme-butch reader*. New York: Alyson Publications.

Peterson, C. (2013). The lies that bind: Heteronormative constructions of 'family' in social work discourse. *Journal of Gay and Lesbian Social Services*, 25(4), 486–508.

Plante, R.F. & Maurer, L.M. (eds.) (2010). *Doing gender diversity: Readings in theory and real-world experience*. Boulder: Westview Press/Perseus.

Rimmerman, C.A. & Wilcox, C. (eds.) (2007). *The politics of same-sex marriage*. Chicago: University of Chicago Press.

Rubano, C. (2015). Where do the mermaids stand? Toward a 'gender-creative pastoral sensibility'. *Pastoral Psychology*. http://link.springer.com/article/10.1007%2Fs11089-015-0680-2#/page-1.

Shelley, M. (1869). *Frankenstein: Or the modern Prometheus*. Boston: Francis Sever & Co.

Shoemaker, D. (2007). Pink tornados and volcanic desire: Lois Weaver's resistant femme(nini)tease' in 'Faith and dancing: Mapping femininity and other natural disasters'. *Text and Performance Quarterly*, 27(4), 317–333.

Solnit, R. (2014). *The faraway nearby*. New York: Penguin.

Stewart, K. (2007). *Ordinary affects*. Durham, NC: Duke University Press.

Stryker, S. (2006). My words to Victor Frankenstein above the village of Chamounix: Performing transgender rage. In Stryker, S. & Whittle, S., eds., *The transgender studies reader*, pp. 244–251. New York: Routledge.

Woolf, V. (1929/2015). *A room of one's own and three guineas*. Ed. Snaith, A. New York: Oxford University Press.

Ziv, A. (2014). Girl meets boy: Cross-gender queer sex and the promise of pornography. *Sexualities*, 17(7), 885–905.

6

QUEERING MEMORY

b.

My grandmother's adopted name was Bernice. Her middle initial was b; the letter a placeholder for an absent birth name. A name my grandmother was called, but no longer knew, not when I asked her. And not now, after her death. Still, names have the power to summon. Adoptees and poets know this. Speaking the names of the lost, the forgotten, the dead conjures bodies—eyes like mine, hands like mine—and loves—music, water, animals, oranges.

The b in my grandmother's name is a memory—a lexical trace of the absence and presence in her adoption story (Holman Jones 2005); her disappeared first name a signature of a failure to belong and to remember. She was adopted when she was young, a baby, but no longer an infant. Her adoptive parents—my great-grandparents—took her and her older brother. They wanted a boy and a girl, a matched set to love and to do chores on the farm. Or was it the other way around? Her younger brother, Jimmy—though this is not his given name either—was adopted by another family. My grandmother found Jimmy when she was older. They had an on-again, off-again relationship: on when Jimmy needed a place to stay and pocket money, off when he moved on to some other state, some other job, some new marriage. Finally they just lost track of each other. Each time my grandmother told this story, I ask if she knows where Jimmy is now. She says somewhere in California. I ask my grandmother if she wants to find Jimmy again. I ask her if she wants to find what's missing in her life's story. She shakes her head. No.

No Place Like Home

Being adopted is a life woven out of threads of outsiderness, shame, guilt, embodiment, memory and most of all, a yearning for home. Though our home is not the same home that others talk about, and love is not the same love that majoritarian people enjoy; home and love are contingent, illusive and often (if not always) disappointing. For adoptees, home and love (like family) are also simultaneously virtual and actual: actual because we do make vital connections and virtual because home and love often feel elsewhere, just outside of reach.

For queer people, sexuality is also virtual and actual: actual because bodies meet, and virtual because we are still outside of straight society, despite recent legislative progress in some times and places and only for some individuals. Queer sex and gender is situational: it remains intelligible in certain contexts, invisible or unintelligible in others. Trans★ may be more visible now than ever before, but non-binary lives, sexualities and genders remain relatively invisible. Aging queer bodies, passions and lives are more invisible still. Being adopted and being queer are both what Erin Manning calls "a quasi-virtual experience: actual because all steps actually take place, virtual because all the microperceptions of pastness and futurity are enveloped in the becoming-movement" (2009, p. 38). The experience of being adopted and the experience of being queer are 'potentialities'—always on the horizon, always searching for a future in and out of past and present belongings. It is the experience of building families and home by thinking through a 'structure of missing' out (Manning 2013, p. 105; Probyn 1995, p. 83).

★

I consider how I got here: I pushed through the adoption paperwork, repeating the motions of a linguistic gestation: photographs, certified letters, figures and fingerprints. I pushed against the ticking clock of my heart, my hands, my mind. I read all the books written by adult transnational adoptees. And what I read makes me fall in on myself, unable to stop looking, unable to sleep at night: I read how families and identities are lost and destroyed in the quest to manufacture a steady stream of available orphans through a "clean break" on the way to a "better life." How married couples become single birth mothers, temporary choices become fabricated relinquishments, and given names become generic nomenclature meant to sterilize an exchange of human beings. How being shipped a world away (or next door) to be raised by people who do not look like you, or speak your mother tongue, or share your blood or your bonds *feels*. How returning to a birthplace where you look but do not look like you belong, speak but do not speak the language, and feel but do not feel one with your family creates a chasm of loneliness so complete it can never be filled. How longing becomes the human currency exchanged for international aid, military support and economic development. How barren middle-class white women eager to meet the demands of compulsory parenthood pay the wages of this exchange (Holman Jones 2011). I read myself. I read her.

★

Watching the film *Lion*, an autobiographic story in which a child becomes lost and therefore adopted, I cried for the protagonist's feeling of joy when he did find home. Or maybe I cried for myself, because I never have.

> I cried when he found his mother, *of course*, because of the agonizing
> sorrow I felt when my mother would not let me find her.
> I could never find that embrace.
> I could never find a mother's love in her open arms.
> I could never find a community to welcome me back without
> ambivalence.
> I did find my birth family and the humiliation of begging them to meet
> me was mitigated by a brief and singular opening
> and then quickly closed over like a scar,
> closed but never gone.
> Scar tissue remains weaker than original skin.
>
> In fairness, I did the leaving.
> I have done the leaving all my life.
> It is too painful to be left—annihilating.
> Being left by my birthmother is my primal wound[1];
> I am not able to allow it a second time.
> And yet, after all my years of work, after forcing myself on them,
> they were semi-friendly and then that was it.
> They did not pursue me.
> They never said, "Hey why did you move to Australia?" They never said,
> "We can stay in touch anyway."
> None of them—not one of them—stayed in touch.
>
> My ideas of love and intimacy are formed by experiences like
> these extremes.
> I can watch *Lion* and say it's just a movie, but I weep knowing it represents
> my experience. That's why we cry in movies—because they are more than
> just a story.
> My own feelings of abandonment
> are juxtaposed with my adoptive mother Anna Mae's enmeshment
> with me.
> I have both the sorrow of my birthmother's rejection
> and the expectation that everyone will love me as fiercely as Anna Mae.

So it—so I—oscillate between extremes of total rejection/abjection and total symbiosis.

Where does desire come in? Desire is an extension of the intimacy and abjection of being cast out, and for adoptees this casting out is evidenced in our bodies, our stories, our social context.
How do we 'get back' to love, to attachment, to intimacy? Desire. Pleasure.

My feelings of abandonment coexist with a kind of passion that is more like a survival strategy.
It's not a hole that never fills, it's worse than that.
If it was just a hole, maybe I'd be an addict, or a recluse,
or dead (like my brother Michael).

Though somewhere even the wrong kind of love stopped, or changed.
Maybe I changed.
A kind of love that feels good to a child isn't always right for an adult.
Since about 20 I've been looking for something from other people
I can't find.
Never good enough, always disappointing.
Even not-enough love feels like annihilation to me, it's true.
It's difficult to live with, that kind of never-enoughness. For me, and them.
I don't think people remember or understand what it's like to not belong to a tribe. It is not a historical pain. It's like pneumonia; it hurts every single time I inhale.
Catches me off guard.
It's like never knowing what might come.
Like when I'm away from home, out on the street or travelling or whatever?
And then I arrive home and that feeling of just . . . exhaling?
That feeling of arriving to your own home, your own safe space, where you can just *be*?
I don't think adoptees know that space.
Some adoptees build their own tribe through sheer force of will, but does that mean we trust it? I don't think so.
It's hard to know whether one can build it for one's self, or whether it has to be given. It's like giving yourself an award—it's just not the same.
I experience extreme feelings of powerless, maybe because of this inability to find or create my home. My safe place. I go out looking for it in the world, but it's not that kind of thing.
Sometimes I fantasize about having my own safe space, my tribe, my place of irrefutable belonging.
Because then what power would anyone else have?
I would already be home. And no one could take it away.

★

I read and I write. I write so that someday she might read my words and understand—what? That I thought that love might make loss bearable? That I love her not because I couldn't have children of my *own*, but because she is not mine, because children are never someone's to own. If I wasn't her mother, who would be? If I'm not her mother, who or what will occupy the cavern filled by my love? Who will make and offer her a home?

And then I wonder whether the world needs one more page filled with the grief and shame of one more adoptive parent. I wonder if the world needs one more story of an adoptive mother trying to understand her own desires, her own love, her own losses. If you are adopted, a hush falls around you. Decisions are made about which stories to tell and which to keep silent, what to reveal and what to keep sealed. This hush is a pact, an exchange of messy silences for something tangible and predictable: a family. A home. You tell yourself as loss and lose yourself in the telling: I am adopted.

Or so I am told.

Decisions about who to tell and what to say are made when there is seamlessness to incorporation and identification; when you look and act the part—a member of the family, at home. In fact there is no need at all to lie about adoptees' origins, but we do. No need beyond respect for the adoptive parents, their investment. Their desire to not be undermined by the truth. But why does their truth override the others in the adoption triad?

When you don't look the part—when you're too dark or too fair to fit—your story becomes public, subject to interpretation. This story is also a pact; an unarticulated exchange of what is *natur*al for what is *right*: the natural needs of often abandoned, often poor, often dark-skinned children are bartered against the rights of often childless, often affluent, often light-skinned parents. The naturalness of a child's belonging—to a person and to a place—strains against the rightness of assimilation and wholeness. Beginnings are erased and origins are abandoned in exchange for an 'as if' family, a linguistic bloodline. A storybook love.

Or so I am told.

What's Missing

Jeanette Winterson, an adoptee herself, writes that "adopted children are self-invented because we have to be; there is an absence, a void, a question mark at the very beginning of our lives. A crucial part of our story is gone, and violently, like a bomb in the womb" (2012, p. 5). And so a story must be invented and told, over and over again, so that a child becomes possible in the mirror dance of self and mother, birthright and family, body and memory. We are all told into being—the narrative of our lives creates the "'reality-effect' of a child, a self and an identity" (Winterson 2012, p. 5; Pollock 1999, p. 69). But adoption drops you into this story after it has begun—it's "like reading a book with the first few pages missing.

It's like arriving after curtain up. The feeling that something is missing never, ever leaves you—and it can't, and it shouldn't, because something *is* missing" (Winterson 2012, p. 5). In this story, an adopted child can become the something missing—faded into the kinds of normalizing and replicating birth stories that are "always already told . . . pressed flat into the pages of family memory" (Pollock 1999, p. 65). And in that absence we—and those we encounter—sometimes invent stories to make up for the ones that are lost.

★

I've spent a lifetime searching for those missing pages; in my twenties, I searched for them sitting across from my therapist Irna, an extraordinary surrogate mother, confessor and friend. As a native New Yorker, I see therapy as an onion, not a sprint: there are always more layers to be peeled away. Well, peeled back if not exactly away. As a teenager, I participated in family therapy when my eldest brother caused us all collective harm. Despite its lack of measurable success, I found that I loved the talking cure, and have returned to it regularly throughout my life at times of expansive self-exploration, or at times of crisis.

In my mid-twenties, in response to rising feelings of distress associated with being adopted, I began to see Irna. While at university, I went for my ten free sessions, and when they were over I wanted to continue. The university therapist recommended that I look for the person who would be right for me. She told me that any therapist worth their weight would not mind being 'interviewed' and in the end I interviewed six different therapists before I settled on Irna. I chose her because I asked her (flippantly, I thought) how she would feel when, inevitably, I would dump her and (probably unexpectedly) walk away. She looked me straight in the eye and said, "I take your statement as a challenge—a test—and I want to assure you that I will do everything in my power to keep you here when your feelings of overwhelm cause you to try to walk away." I loved Irna from that moment forward and saw her every week for six years.

I was searching for my birthmother in New York State, where all adoption records were (and still are) legally closed. After years of searching on my own and with the help of friends, after years of petitioning the government and my adoption agency Catholic Charities and attending an adoptee support group in the apartment of legendary foundling and New York adoption community legend Joe Sol, I finally decided to pay an anonymous person on Long Island to find my birthmother. It was both an exciting and ultimately crushing experience. While the logistics of that search unfolded outside of Irna's rooms, inside we met weekly (and sometimes more) to try to keep me going through the nearly-unbearable and heartbreaking experience of rejection and aloneness my adoption search brought up for me.

One day, full of despair, I was reluctant to leave Irna's office. I wasn't speaking much but she, equally reluctant to kick me out, sat patiently. Unaware, I must have been looking up periodically, desperate for connection but not sure how to manage it. Finally Irna spoke:

"Sometimes when I think about you and our sessions here, I wonder what it must have been like for you in the orphanage. I imagine you laying in your crib, from birth to six months old, which is such a terribly long time, developmentally. I think of you laying there, and the nuns of Catholic Charities walking back and forth in the long rooms full of babies and children, trying to care for you but undoubtedly understaffed. I imagine the economy of that place was that, like all places, those who could manage to demand the attention, who were able to attract care and contact and touch, were the ones who thrived. I imagine you there among others like you, somehow in some intuitive human way, knowing this, and figuring out how to get the attention of those caregivers. As a pre-verbal infant, all you would have had, I imagine, was your eyes."

I looked up, then, at Irna, tears streaming down my face, some kind of recognition ignited. "I don't know, maybe."

She smiled with care. "I think of how you must have demanded attention, then had to continue holding them, with your fierce eyes, the way you do with me, here. Sometimes in our sessions I feel held by your eyes. They are inescapable, intense. I think often about why that might be so, and how those eyes have kept you alive, even when words have failed you."

Adoption Story

My daughter wants to hear, over and over again, the story of when she came to be my daughter. It's not a birth story, in the sense of her—a child—inhabiting my—a mother's—story, "shaping it from the inside out . . . the mother's story pregnant with the child's own," recalling the "first rites of separation (pushing, expelling, cutting, weighing, testing, wrapping, removing)" (Pollock 1999, p. 69). No. This is the adoption story, which comes after the first rites, the first (missing) pages, the first separation, expelling, cutting, removing. This is the story of her arrival in America—another expelling, weighing and wrapping and the long flight from Korea and into my arms. Come to think of it, it's not unlike a birth story, though I am outside of it, waiting at the other end of the long tunnel in the arrivals lounge at JFK airport, waiting for a glimpse of her. This is the adoption story, and her favorite part is the part about the camera.

When I tell the story, I begin at the beginning, for me, telling the story of my grandmother's adoption, the history of that missing story in the memory of my family. I begin with my reading and writing and waiting to become her mother. I begin with these parts of the story, but what she wants to hear is the missing part—the part about the camera.

> I am waiting at the other end of the long tunnel in the arrivals lounge at JFK airport.

> I am waiting for a glimpse of her.
> I am waiting with the camera in my hands, feet planted, ready to take a
> photograph of her the first time I see her. I want to document her arrival,
> so she will have something to hold onto from those first few moments,
> not of her life or her story, but my telling of when our relation
> came to be.

I am waiting with the camera in my hands, feet planted, and then I see her—at least I think it's her, but from so far away I don't recognize her as the child I know from the pictures I've been carrying in my pocket since the day they—and she— arrived in my life.

Still, I think it's her, the baby I see through the viewfinder of the camera. She is held aloft by an adoption agency social worker who is walking side by side with another adoption agency social worker holding aloft another Korean baby being adopted today, in-flight siblings on that long transnational passage.

I press the button, taking two blurry shots of the baby I think is her before dropping the camera on the floor and running toward her—my arms stretched out to receive the baby I think is her—from the adoption agency social worker. There are other photos from later that day, but the story of her arrival, the moment our relation came to be, are not contained in the two fuzzy images I took before dropping the camera and running. That part, that important moment in our past, is blurry, missing. Gone.

This story, the adoption story, is not *the* missing part, the missing past. Though the story of her mother and her father and her birth is just as fuzzy, just as blurry. What we know of *that* story is the narrative we piece together from the "Parent Information" sheet slipped in behind her medical records and supplied by the adoption agency social worker. What we know is this: her mother is young, just 18, and lives with the grandmother who raised *her* after her parents abandoned her for no known reason. Her mother works in a factory in a small rural town in South Korea. Her mother dated her father, who is older than she is by 10 years and who works in a small store and plays the piano, for only a few months. By the time her mother discovered she was pregnant, the relationship was over. She does not tell the father about the baby; instead her mother makes arrangements with the social welfare organization to place her for adoption. Her mother receives free medical care and gives birth in a hospital in Seoul. Her mother signs the relinquishment papers and leaves the hospital. Three days later she leaves too, in the arms of the foster mother who will care for her until the long journey to America five months later.

Like a Kind of Braille

She does not ask me to tell her the story of her birth parents. Instead, she becomes *the one who tells*, inventing her own story (Pollock 1999, p. 70). In this story, her mother is still young, still raised by her grandmother, still abandoned by her parents, still works in a factory. But her father is gone, though not completely. He is still older, still works in a small store, and still plays the piano. But when he hears her mother is pregnant, when he learns about *her*, he walks away. *He walks away, walks away*. This is how she tells it, the story of her birth parents. When she gets to the part about her father and him walking away, I used to correct her. Used to pull out the "Parent Information" sheet and say, "Look, here, it doesn't say that your father walked away. It says he didn't know about you. Only that." I'd correct her and the next time she'd tell the story of her birth parents, she'd return to her telling. When she'd get to the part about her father, she'd say, over and over again, "He walks away. He walks away, walks away."

In her story, the missing part and the missing past is "the fossil record, the imprint of another life" (Guay 2015). I used to think her telling blurred or distorted the story, though in every retelling, she returns to what's missing and what might have been. Her story writes the life that she can never have, and in each retelling, her words "trace the space where it might have been," moving across the missing parts like a kind of Braille. Her story says, "There are markings here, raised like welts. Read them. Read the hurt. Rewrite them. Rewrite the hurt" (Guay 2015). Ana Maria Guay (2015) writes of the pressure so many of us—adoptive parents, social workers, siblings, extended family—put on adoptees to feel and be grateful for their adoptions, despite their hurts and losses and grief. She says, "We invent ourselves around pain, displacement, and anger like skin growing numb around a scar. Be grateful? For this?" (Guay 2015).

Toxic Gratitude

It's taboo to be an ungrateful or grieving adoptee; it is also taboo to express the sorrow of the adoptive mother. Each feels and offers a kind of love that is never, ever good enough. That sorrow, that ungratefulness, that wrong kind of love are not the stuff of adoption narratives. And the pain, anger and fear adoptees—and queer people—feel are not the stories we want to be telling. We do not want to be—still, always, again—questioning the racism, nationalism, homophobia and classism of a multimillion dollar adoption industry (Nebeling Peterson & Myong 2015; Guay 2015; Posocco 2014; Park Nelson 2009) and we do not want to be calling out the dismissals, denials and discriminations that happen to queer people every day in the name of 'kin' and family. And yet we do—we must—because these erasures and violences punctuate our everyday. We tell these stories as an antidote to the 'toxic gratitude' expected of adoptees and queer people (Guay 2015; Harris 2014). We tell these stories because "Love, in whatever form, should not be a blank check. The expectation of gratitude is too often rooted in toxic power dynamics between the powerful who demand thanks and the marginalized that are expected to give it" (Guay 2015).

★

When I was a teenager and insisted on privacy, my mother would say, "I made you. I know what you look like." When I didn't obey, my mother would say, "I brought you into this world, and I can take you out." She created me, carried me; I was *hers*, as she too belonged to her mother.

I am standing so many years later in nearly the same kitchen, in nearly the same posture, arguing. My daughter, now a teenager, is mouthy, defiant and loud. I am angry, frustrated and weepy. Though in this fight, I can't tell her the things my mother told me; I didn't make her, I didn't bring her into the world. And I can't take her out. Instead, I ask the questions adopted children are always asked: what if I hadn't adopted you? Where would you be now, without my love? What kind of life would you have had, full of loneliness and longing? What I don't—or can't—ask is who pays the wages of this exchange.

She says the things that most teenagers say—what a dear friend who also has a teenager at home calls 'sucker punches to the soul'[2]: words so unexpected, so swift, you don't know what hit you: You're a terrible mother. You don't know how to have fun, and you don't want anyone else to, either. I hate you.

And she says things that many, maybe most—you're not sure—adopted children say, at some moment or another. These, too, are sucker punches to the soul, and they hit me so hard they take my breath away: I wish you'd never adopted me. Oh, wait. I wish you'd never bought me. Maybe you can return me and get your money back. You're pathetic. A failure. Not even a mother. I hate you.

I consider how I got here, what belongs to me. I consider what's worse, the bad mothers I invent for her or the ones she invents for herself (Winterson 2012, p. 220). The pain of what she doesn't know or the shame of what I do. I am not sure whether to laugh or to cry.

Feeling Backwards

For adopted kids and queer kids, shame accrues like the debris washed up on the beach after a thunderstorm—tangled, messy, smelly. We struggle alone to find 'others like us' and also 'acceptance'—a rolling project that starts with self-acceptance (which itself can take a lifetime) and then moves out to others and other publics. This is no small feat. It can be a full-time job, and it can end so unsuccessfully, crushed under the weight and repercussions of this 'coming to consciousness' that many of us do not make it, like my dear brother Michael.

If and when we reach some level of acceptance, both internal and hopefully then relational, we know that the process of 'coming out' never ends: a great shock to many queers, who think it is something they have to go through in the beginning and then will mercifully be over (Guittari 2014). For adoptees, too, coming out is never over. Instead, we return to the scene of the first separation, the first telling, however fraught, however fuzzy, however shattering, looking for what's missing, trying to recover what's gone (Love 2007, p. 45). Queer subjects and adoptees recognize the ambivalent and negative possibilities of recovering the past.

In *Feeling Backwards*, Heather Love (2007) writes that while historians imagine "that no one would search out the roots of his or her identity if that history were not positive," gay and lesbian historiographers also recognize how

> negative or ambivalent identifications with the past can serve to disrupt the present. Making connections with historical losses or with images of ruined or spoiled identity in the past can set into motion a gutting "play of recognitions," another form of effective history.
>
> *(p. 45)*

That's the thing about returning to the site of trauma, searching for a way to restore or re-story the fiction of what should have been ours—acceptance, connection, family: it happens over and over again. These returns are melancholic, marked by the desire to "uncover an anterior connection, a saturnine quality embedded in chronology that hopes to enter a different, fulfilled register of time" (Caputi 2005, p. 28). Though for adoptees and for queer people, a return to the "retrograde backwards pull of melancholia" might just make something reparative and powerful out of the missing past (Shahani 2012, p. 42), however painful, however shattering (Love 2007, p. 45). And so we keep coming back.

★

The family is gathered around my grandmother's hospital bed. One of her doctors enters and turns off the machines, one by one. In the silence, I hear a faint clicking sound. A falling, a snapping, a door slamming shut.

I float into the waiting room and hover there until someone says it's time to go. In the car, I sit in the back seat with my daughter, clutching her small hand. "I lied to you earlier," my mother says from the front seat.

"What?"

"I lied."

"About what?"

"I lied when I said I didn't tell your grandmother about you being a lesbian. I lied when I said your grandmother wouldn't have understood."

I consider the queer sensation of becoming possible in confession not to a lie, but to a truth; of a transformation figured in silence.

I consider, again, how I got here: If mothers and children are not possessions and if our most intimate connections are never choices we can wholly make or unmake, perhaps what could count is not who but *how* we love one another.

I don't know whether to laugh or to cry.

I know there is a price for telling the truth about ourselves, for naming and narrating myself as recognizable in and through time. There is a price because we fail to belong and to remember. There is a price because we change.

We change again and again, losing and finding and "risking ourselves precisely at moments of unknowingness," precisely when our willingness to speak ourselves creates our very "chance of becoming" (Butler 2005, p. 136).

Or so I am told.

Staying Gone

The adoption return experience—if it happens at all—is often about meeting strangers who are supposed to be family and then enduring the awkward getting-to-know-you phase, which almost always consists of them asking what you have done with your life. The questions inexorably begin with 'are you married, do you have children?' and I don't know how it *can't* be disappointing to come out as queer at that point, unless of course you have a queer birth family, which is highly improbable. The queer return for an adoptee is a kind of precarity, a relational and social condition of dependency, need and exposure, in which some of us are viewed as disposable, deprived of "even knowing what space one can call home" (Butler in Puar et al. 2012, pp. 163, 168). Judith Butler points out that no one "escapes the precarious dimension of social life—it is, we might say, our common non-foundation. Nothing 'founds' us outside of a struggle to establish bonds that sustain us" (Butler in Puar et al. 2012, p. 170).

For adoptees, the 'flawed or frayed' social bonds some experience are lost, irre-coverable, subject to a kind of decay (Butler in Puar et al. 2012, p. 169). It is the decay of the trope of 'going home.' Decaying because it grew for a time, and then that growing is abandoned, is reversed. Precarious because it is a plank upon which you march out your heart, begging someone who has no experience of you to love you and to take you 'back,' back to a place from which you have never really come, only perhaps in stories. The exchange starts from the understanding that returned adoptees' bodies and stories represent a kind of rupture, an embodi-ment of failure, and the pain of return. This is the dislocating, disorienting loss of bearings that Elspeth Probyn (2015) describes as the "pain of the return" the "proper definition of nostalgia," joining the Greek *nostos* and *algia* "to signify 'a painful yearning to return home'" (p. 114). The queer adoptee who *returns* knows herself to be an artifact of fear, grief, shame: of the birth parents' (usually mother's) own failure and shame. And in their shame, the birth parent can never see the adoptee as an individual. In this exchange of queer forgetting, their desire (even if unstated, unrealized) is for us just to 'stay gone.'

Sitting on the Stoop

It's unseasonably cold in San Jose; still, I sit on her stoop while my girlfriend waits around the corner in a rental car. 'Sitting on the stoop' here used as both truth and fiction, past and present. I am thirty years old and have traveled from New York, spurred on by a stranger's words that I am 'daughter' to this 'mother.' I want to see her, just once.

She hides behind the curtains, behind a closed front door, and turns up the television.

"Go away!" she yells.

Her husband, Tony, mumbles, "Don't be like that, Dorothy."

Silence.

Light San Jose breeze.

Kids playing on the next street.

"Open the door," I say flatly, "You might as well open the door."

"Go away," she says again, like a mantra, like a plea. "You're a ghost and I want you to leave."

"I'm not leaving!" I shout. "And I'm not a ghost."

There's a ruffling of the curtains near her front door, and I see a plump face with round glasses.

"That's cheating!" I yell. "If I can't see you, you can't see me!" and I turn my back to her but refuse to leave.

The standoff continues.

"I'll call the cops!" she yells.

"Do it. What are you gonna tell them, your daughter is on your stoop?"

Silence. Her neighbor looks out his front door.

She keeps shifting from one window to the next, peeping out until I look up, then pulling away.

"You're a ghost and I want you to leave."

"I'm not a ghost," I say, but she doesn't hear me. No one hears me.

"I'm not a ghost, I'm a person," I say again.

Nothing.

I sit down. For a while I cry. Then I sob. I sit there for five hours, and she never opens the door. Eventually, I decide there is nothing for me in this place, and I return to the rental car where my girlfriend naps, and we drive away.

Queer Return

For adoptees, both fantasy and fact play a role in our self-narratives, our imaginaries of home. What do we have to hold onto if not our stories? If not our memories, however blurry, however out of time, however full of pain? Or terror. However full of what's missing. Probyn (1995) reminds us that "the story of love, loss, longing, desire and missing is told through fragmentary images" (Probyn 1995, p. 82). And when mothers and love and family and a safe space to just be ourselves are missing, starting at the beginning—at birth or place of origins or coming into relation—is an impossible project. It's impossible because even in stories, a life doesn't have a "cause and effect relationship the way we wish it did; it's as arbitrary as the mass of chaotic images we call memory" (Yuknavitch 2011,

p. 32). The stories we tell are a series of "fragments and repetitions and pattern formations . . . put into lines to narrativize over fear" and loss (Yuknavitch 2011, p. 32).

Though whatever reparative or restorative (re-*storyative*) power such fragments might hold, hinges on a break from the ever-forward, ever-linear movement of memory and history, of "ordering origins" in an attempt at "creating order from the point of beginning" (Probyn 2015, p. 113). It is to this place—the place of missing and the limits of memory—that we return.

★

I visit my mother in spring, the time of year for gathering, fruitfulness, possibility.

No. That's not quite right. *We* visit my parents because you remind, remark, insist: my parents are getting old; my father's health is fragile nine years on from the stroke. And my mother isn't getting any younger, either.

We make the overseas flight, catch the domestic flight from the coast to the center, then drive the rest of the way. I, the daughter who is absent on each and every holiday, big and small, return. I turn up on the doorstep, on Mother's Day. My own daughter stays home in Australia, thousands of miles away.

This will be one of only a handful of trips I've made home since I came out. It will be only the second time I've brought a lover. The first visit, not long after I left my husband and moved into a place of my own with my daughter, didn't go badly, but it didn't go well, either. It was: she's so different from you, so young. It was: it looks like you've taken someone else in, to love, to tend to. Or was it the other way around?

We turn up, you and I, on the stoop and ring the bell. We stand there, listening to the low mumble of the television and dogs barking inside. We wait. But I know, with a certainty you have never had, that my mother will open the door. Just as I know the twin sorrows of rejection and love—enfleshed and enacted by the mother who will open that door—does open that door. She ushers us in with hugs and admonitions about where we've been—all day, all year, all along.

Still, we don't have long—just two days—the short visit that I insisted upon. Enough time to talk and maybe connect, but not enough time to fight or feel the immeasurable grief that has marked our exchanges all along. Or so I think. Or maybe just hope.

We make our introductions, share a meal and shuffle off to bed downstairs—into the overstuffed basement fitted out with a leaky air mattress and flannel sheets. We sit facing each other on the inflatable mattress, sinking down little by little, and marvel at the familiar similarities of our surroundings. You tell me what things—most everything we lay our eyes on—would have been in your childhood home. Were there. That clock, this vase, those recliners, these framed photographs. The stuff of a family, artifacts of growing up in late 20th-century America that seem gone to you now—save the few small things packed up and sent to you across the ocean after your mother died. Suddenly they—and that not-so-long ago home and family—are here. Again. Returned to you in the home of my mother.

★

But as the saying goes, you can never go home. Can never return to the home and family you once (or should have) had. "Or rather, once returned, you realize the cliché that home is never what it was" (Probyn 2015, p. 114).

And still, we return, again. And again. And we revisit the stories that tell us in all of our fragmentation and missing parts. Why? "The point is . . . to rewind our stories but not to recount them as links in a chronological chain that ties the present to a fixed past" (Probyn 2015, p. 115). To return as a kind of feeling back- wards, a kind of "thinking through a structure of missing" (Probyn 1995, p. 83), which recalls how mothers and children, how memory and love miss each other, and how this missing serves to produce a certain affective spatiality"—one that is "virtual as well as actual" (Manning 2009, p. 38). This missing—of love and moth- ers and home and memory—is "drenched in the immediacy of past and present pain; it is also the stuff out of which we seek to construct the possible" (Probyn 2015, p. 117). Or so we're told.

Notes

1   The title of Nancy Verrier's 1993 book on adoption from the adoptee's point of view—largely viewed as one of the first texts to acknowledge the damaging effects of the trauma of separation from birth mothers that creates feelings of abandonment and loss and painful difficulties in attachment and bonding for adopted children.
2   We thank Deanna Shoemaker for this phrase and its powerful descriptive force it holds for these, and other, stories.

References

Butler, J. (2005). *Giving an account of oneself.* New York: Fordham University Press.

Caputi, M. (2005). *A kinder, gentler America: Melancholia and the mythical 1950s.* Minneapolis: University of Minnesota Press.

Guay, A.M. (2015). 'Suffer the little children' adoption and toxic gratitude. *The Toast.* http://the-toast.net/2015/11/19/adoption-and-toxic-gratitude/

Guittari, N. (2014). *Coming out: The new dynamics.* Boulder, CO: FirstForumPress.

Harris, A. (2014). Ghost-child. In Wyatt, J. & Adams, T.E., eds., *On writing families: Autoethnog-raphies of presence and absence, love and loss,* pp. 69–75. Rotterdam, The Netherlands: Sense.

Holman Jones, S. (2005). (M)othering loss: Telling adoption stories, telling performativity. *Text and Performance Quarterly,* 25(2), 113–135.

Holman Jones, S. (2011). Lost and found. *Text and Performance Quarterly,* 31(4), 322–341.

Love, H. (2007). *Feeling backward: Loss and the politics of queer history.* Cambridge, MA: Har-vard University Press.

Manning, E. (2009). *Relationscapes: Movement, art, philosophy.* Cambridge, MA: MIT Press.

Manning, E. (2013). *Always more than one: Individuation's dance.* Durham, NC: Duke Uni-versity Press.

Nebeling Peterson, M. & Myong, L. (2015). (Un)liveabilities: Homonationalism and transnational adoption. *Sexualities*, 18(3), 329–345.

Park Nelson, K. (2009). *Mapping multiple histories of Korean American transnational adoption*. Washington, DC: US Korea Institute.

Probyn, E. (1995). Lesbians in space: Gender, sex and the structure of missing. *Gender, Place & Culture*, 2(1), 77–84.

Probyn, E. (2015). *Outside belongings*. New York: Routledge.

Pollock, D. (1999). *Telling bodies performing birth: Everyday narratives of childbirth*. New York: Columbia University Press.

Posocco, S. (2014). On the queer necropolitics of transnational adoption in Guatemala. In Haritaworn, J.M., Kuntsman, A. & Posocco, S., eds., *Queer necropolitics*. New York: Routledge.

Puar, J., Berlant, L., Butler, J., Cvjic, B., Lorey, I. & Vujanovic, A. (2012). Precarity talk: A virtual roundtable with Lauren Berlant, Judith Butler, Bojana Cvjic, Isabell Lorey, Kasbir Puar, and Ana Vujanovic. *TDR: The Drama Review*, 56(4), 163–177.

Shahani, N. (2012). *Queer retrosexualities: The politics of reparative return*. Lanham, MD: Lehigh University Press.

Verrier, N. (1993). *The primal wound: Understanding the adopted child*. Baltimore, MD: Gateway Press.

Winterson, J. (2012). *Why be happy when you could be normal?* London: Vintage.

Yuknavitch, L. (2011). *Chronology of water: A memoir*. Portland: Hawthorne Books.

INDEX